THE DRACULA SYNDROME

THE DRACULA SYNDROME

Richard Monaco and
William Burt

HEADLINE

First published in Great Britain in 1993
by HEADLINE BOOK PUBLISHING

10 9 8 7 6 5 4 3 2 1

British Library Cataloguing in Publication Data

Monaco, Richard
Dracula Syndrome
I. Title II. Burt, William
133.423

ISBN 0-7472-0928-6

Typeset by
Letterpart Limited, Reigate, Surrey

Printed and bound in Great Britain by
Mackays of Chatham PLC, Chatham, Kent

HEADLINE BOOK PUBLISHING
A division of Hodder Headline PLC
Headline House
79 Great Titchfield Street
London W1P 7FN

CONTENTS

THE CULT VAMPIRE

ILLUSTRATIONS

INTRODUCTION

Vampires have enthralled readers, theatre- and cinema-goers for centuries. The most famous fictional creation is Bram Stoker's classic *Dracula*, written more than a century ago. Since then, vampires have been an inexhaustible topic; people can't get enough information about their bizarre secret world.

The film and TV industry reported that in 1992–3 there were more vampire-oriented productions launched than at any other time in its history. The best of these was Francis Ford Coppola's faithful rendition of Stoker's *Dracula*. But these are all stories, the stuff that nightmares are made of. What about the vampires who walk among us today – real-life killers – latter-day Draculas with an insatiable appetite for human blood? These are characters guaranteed to make your skin crawl in a way unsurpassed by skilled film monsters such as Bela Lugosi and Christopher Lee. And, as we shall prove, they exist.

This is not as improbable as you may think.

In this dark hall of fame of twentieth-century vampires, you will be introduced to and chilled by flesh-and-blood criminals who have prowled and preyed on helpless victims. Some are still alive and well, but all have one thing in common: a compelling lust for the taste of human blood. Interestingly, our modern vampires come in all shapes and sizes and from all walks of life. Incredibly, very few of them were ever judged insane in a court of law. Nor did many of them ever offer apologies or express regret for their weird lifestyles.

Sweet Mary Lensfield made her living translating children's books in the 1930s. But her lifestyle belied the strange secret of this demure vampire – she had an uncontrollable urge to drink blood, a habit she picked up while a student at Vassar.

In 1990, in the backwoods town of Junin, Peru, a twenty-one-year-old would-be vampire, Octavio Flores, was too scared of AIDS to stalk victims – so he frequently slashed his wrists and drank his *own* blood. Over a period of months he nearly drank himself dry and ended up hospitalized for acute anaemia.

Joggers should beware of vampires: a San Francisco college student out for an early-morning jog in August 1987 reported that he was kidnapped by a burly vampire who dragged him into his van, which was decked out like a torture chamber on wheels, and held him captive for an hour, all the time drinking his blood. The student, who escaped after stabbing his attacker with a screwdriver, remembers the ceiling of the van bore a poster of a pentagram, a symbol used in Satanic rituals.

Some people associate vampires with the erotic, rather than with sociopathic violence. According to a recent poll conducted by Dr Stephen Kaplan who heads the New York-based Vampire Research Center, eighty per cent of American women polled said they would have sex with a vampire if the opportunity ever arose. We think reading this book will radically alter that statistic. Dr Kaplan's frequently quoted Research Center has a wealth of information about real-life people who practise vampirism for kicks.

There are even tales of modern-day vampirism which would be amusing if the subject matter wasn't so repugnant, such as the story of Bobby Lester. Police launched a full-scale man-hunt in 1990 before they finally arrested Miami's Biting Bandit, Bobby Lester, who chomped his way through more than a dozen robbery victims before he was caught. As he mugged them, he bit chunks out of them!

Among the types of vampire you will find: the psychopathic vampire, the vampire pervert, the cult vampire and the benign vampire.

The Psychopathic Vampire
These are frenzied, bloodlusting sadists driven by delusions and sexual frenzy – maniacal Jack the Rippers who can only find orgasmic release and satisfaction by drawing or drinking human blood.

A prime example is the Canadian Vampire, Wayne Boden, who began his bloodlust in the 1970s. A presentable young bachelor, he felt compelled to bite savagely the breasts of young women to draw blood as he throttled them to death.

In the 1940s, Steve Wilson of Los Angeles developed a thirst for blood only after he had a few drinks. In a drunken, psychopathic frenzy he butchered two unfortunate prostitutes within a twenty-four-hour period.

Also in California, in the same decade, there was the mysterious killer of beautiful, raven-haired Elizabeth Short, an unlucky starlet who fell into the clutches of a night stalker who sliced her body in two and drained all her blood before tossing her tortured remains on a vacant lot in the Los Angeles suburbs.

Quiet, respectable family man Richard Cottingham also developed an insatiable bloodlust which led to the brutal mutilation and killings of vice girls in New York's Times Square red-light district in the 1980s.

The Vampire Pervert

These monsters of the night are more sociopathic than psychopathic. Their bloodlust is not manifested as spontaneous surges of violence. They carefully and coolly choose and stalk their prey. Their outwardly normal appearance and deliberate, calculated acts of sadistic violence make them chillingly more sinister than the psychopaths.

In the 1920s, dapper ladies' man Peter Kurten, the Vampire of Düsseldorf, equated the drawing of blood with the ultimate act of love, as did the Russian monster and former schoolteacher Andrei Chikatilo.

In New York, gentle grandfatherly Albert Fish – at sixty-six the oldest man to die in the electric chair – carefully and methodically selected, stalked and violated hundreds of innocent children to satisfy his bloodlust.

Earlier in the century there was the reign of terror of the aptly named Hungarian, Bela Kiss. A respected businessman, Kiss drank blood and dispatched twenty-seven female victims before vanishing mysteriously, giving rise to an eerie true-vampire legend.

Two unlikely killers of the 1940s were Englishmen John George Haigh and Neville Heath. A polite and refined businessman, Haigh claimed he developed vampire tendencies after being in a car accident. He disposed of his blood-drained victims in an acid bath.

Heath was a distinguished-looking former air force officer and the young women who were his victims fell for his smooth-talking charms. Then he snuffed out their lives to satisfy an inexplicable bloodlust.

The Cult Vampire
These blood-worshipping killers stalk their prey for more esoteric reasons. Some believe blood sacrifices provide them with supernatural powers. Others feel that blood-letting is a necessary ritual to help them achieve their warped goals.

The most infamous vampire-cult killers in recent years hailed from Mexico. In the 1960s, near Monterrey, a blood-drinking sacrificial cult headed by former blonde prostitute turned high priestess Magdalena

Solis butchered dozens of innocent villagers after she declared them unbelievers.

Sophisticated bisexual Adolfo de Jesus Constanzo presided over a weird blood-and-drugs cult that sacrificed as many as fourteen innocent victims in the 1980s. The cult members believed that the spilling of human blood would give them magical powers, including invisibility, and were greatly shocked when the police walked into their lair and handcuffed them.

In the 1980s, all-American mid-western schoolboy Sean Sellers, a Satanic cultist, developed a taste for blood that would lead him to Death Row; young James Riva, from a respectable New England family, heeded mysterious voices which directed him to slay his grandmother with golden bullets before consuming her blood; and Florida computer genius John Crutchley's uncontrollable thirst for blood was satisfied in the goriest way imaginable.

The Benign Vampire
These unfortunates don't fall into the criminal category, and as such are not included in this book, but what is remarkable about such non-lethal blood-stalkers is that, according to our research, there are hundreds, perhaps thousands of people who practise what can only be described as a benign form of vampirism. They simply have a weird thirst for human blood and seldom do they resort to crimes of violence.

Because our focus is the twentieth-century vampire, you

won't find in this book the fourteenth-century Transylvanian sadist Vlad the Impaler (the original Count Dracula), or the infamous Belgian countess Elizabeth de Bathory, who bathed in the blood of thirty young servant-girl victims so she could remain eternally young. For the same reason, even Jack the Ripper doesn't merit a mention in these pages, although he too was undoubtedly impelled to stalk and kill by a vampirish lust for blood and gore.

Most people assume Jack the Ripper was the first blood-hungry night stalker. In fact, more than ten years before old Jack started prowling, a young Frenchman with the unlikely name of Eusebius Pieydagnelle became so obsessed with the smell of blood in the butcher's shop where he worked that he went prowling at nights and slaughtered six women. He admitted that the sight and smell of fresh human blood brought him to orgasm.

There are other fiends of more recent vintage who, one might feel, would warrant inclusion in a book like this. What about mass serial killers Ted Bundy, Henry Lucas, the Hillside Stranglers, Ed Gein (the Wisconsin farmer of the 1950s who is reputedly the role model for the crazy killers made famous in films such as *Psycho*, *The Texas Chainsaw Massacre*, and *The Silence of the Lambs*, among others), and a host of other depraved monsters?

Certainly, they were notorious predators, but in the case of these 'straight' serial killers their primary motivating compulsion was 'the kill' itself, rather than the urge for blood. We have chosen to spotlight only the blood-thirsty in the strictest sense of the word.

So put aside your fictional tales of horror and prepare yourself for the real thing – probably more than you ever dreamed you'd find out about the curse of the vampire which, like Dracula himself, never seems to die.

THE PSYCHOPATHIC VAMPIRE

THE BLACK DAHLIA

Was America's most macabre victim the prey of a vampire?

The sad and brief saga of young Elizabeth Short – better known in US crime annals as 'The Black Dahlia' – has still to be resolved, although there is strong evidence to indicate she fell victim to a twentieth-century vampire.

Although her unsolved murder has been the subject of numerous books and movies, one aspect of the gruesome Black Dahlia slaying has never undergone close scrutiny by murder historians: when her dismembered body was found discarded in two sections like a shattered doll on a vacant lot in Los Angeles in January 1947, both parts had been deliberately and systematically drained of every drop of blood.

Forensic experts who examined her hideously mutilated remains all reached the same conclusion: she had been subjected to perverted blood-draining tortures while she was still alive. There can be little doubt that the twenty-two-year-old raven-haired good-time girl met her death at the hands of a killer with a vampirish bloodlust.

A lovelorn, aimless wanderer, Elizabeth Short went to Hollywood, like many other young hopefuls, with stars in her eyes, but her dreams of becoming a film star didn't work out. She worked hard to attract the attention of casting directors and other influential men in the movie industry. To establish a distinctive personality, she dressed totally in black, right down to her lingerie. Her lustrous black tresses and milky-white skin made her stand out in a town teeming with beautiful young hopefuls.

It was her alluring beauty which spelled her doom, though. Elizabeth attracted men effortlessly. She was a social butterfly, enjoying the attention and generosity of many male admirers. Until that fateful 15 January 1947, when she met Mr Wrong.

She hadn't been seen around for several days before the horrible discovery of her remains on an untidy, rubbish-strewn vacant lot in a Los Angeles suburb by a woman pedestrian who hysterically flagged down a passing police patrol car.

Even tough cops flinched at the gory remains cast aside amid the rubbish like pieces of a doll that had been ripped apart. The body had been hacked in two, obviously after being drained of blood, the upper and lower sections trussed in ropes. As a macabre signature, her killer had carved the initials 'BD' on the fleshy part of one of her thighs – the initials of her Black Dahlia nickname.

When the body was removed to the police morgue for forensic examination, doctors made an even more appalling discovery. The horrible injuries which scarred her hideously mutilated body had obviously been inflicted while she was still alive. Elizabeth Short had been tortured while being drained of her blood, before the killer hacked her torso in two.

The first priority of the murder squad was to establish the identity of the terribly violated young woman – confident that their initial investigation would lead to an early arrest. But the case wasn't to prove that simple.

A native of Medford, Massachusetts, Elizabeth Short came from a broken home. A rebellious teenager, she had run away – to Miami, Florida, where, still only sixteen years old, she celebrated her new-found independence by cavorting on the beaches with handsome young wartime servicemen during the day and working as a waitress at night.

Although under age, she soon gained a reputation in wartime Miami as a hard-drinking party girl. It was her under-age drinking that attracted the attention of Miami police who declared her a juvenile delinquent and gave her a one-way train ticket back home to Massachusetts.

A romantic at heart, young Elizabeth was seeking love. Before she headed back home to Medford in 1944, she thought she had found her dream when she met a handsome young officer, Major Matt Gordon – but her dream was short-lived when her lover returned to action and was killed in a battle arena somewhere in the Far East.

Despondent, disillusioned, but still searching for love and personal success, Elizabeth eventually decided to leave her mother's home once again and seek her fortune in Hollywood this time round. With her fabulous figure, lustrous dark hair and provocative grey-green eyes, she had no trouble signing on with the major studios as an extra. And with the film business thriving during what were industry's golden years, for a while she enjoyed a series of steady, well-paying jobs as a face-in-the-crowd in a number of long-forgotten films.

Always confident that her big break was just over the horizon, Elizabeth began cultivating her 'Black Dahlia' image, dressing alluringly in black all the time. She even wore black jewellery. She relished her new nickname and the notoriety it brought her.

Unfortunately, there was a darker side to her new-found glitzy Tinseltown lifestyle. The casting couch was a way of life for many aspiring young starlets – and the Black Dahlia soon became one of them. She earned a reputation as a sleep-around good-time girl. Perhaps to hide the pain of her sordid lifestyle, young Elizabeth took to the bottle again – this time with a vengeance. Because of the booze and a series of casual one-night stands, her reputation and work as an extra suffered. Jobs at the studios became scarcer and scarcer.

Once again, Elizabeth headed out of town. This time due south, to San Diego, where she resumed her old career as a waitress.

Her drinking habits, however, did not change. It was a drunken binge with a casual boyfriend – later interviewed and cleared by police – that brought her back to Los Angeles, the city of broken dreams. The casual boyfriend was probably the last person to see the Black Dahlia alive. He told police he dropped her off at the

14

Biltmore Hotel in Los Angeles where she had said she was going to meet her sister.

Instead, she was swallowed up by the city until her body was discovered a few days later dismembered and discarded on the vacant suburban lot. To this day, clues are at a premium. Not one single item of her distinctive clothing or jewellery was ever discovered.

Because of the bizarre nature of the murder, it made international headlines. The police received dozens of confessions from men seeking doubtful notoriety – each lead proved to be false.

Then, amid all the crank calls and letters came one promising lead. A city newspaper received a package containing Elizabeth Short's birth certificate, address book and social security card. There was no covering letter. Fingerprints on the envelope turned up a blank at the FBI laboratory.

Detectives were left with the task of combing through the Black Dahlia's address book – again with little or no success.

Meantime, false leads continued to flood into homicide headquarters from all parts of the United States. All turned out to be wild goose chases.

Even today, there are confessions and incredible theories crossing the desks of Los Angeles murder investigators.

Many people subscribe to the theory that she was scooped off the streets by a twentieth-century vampire who wanted her only for her blood. And there is medical speculation that the ropes found on her dismembered body parts were used to suspend her remains aloft while her blood was drained into vats for some demonic vampire's personal consumption.

Some veteran detectives still remain convinced that the address book sent to the Los Angeles newspaper was the only valid clue – and the only direct communication from the killer himself . . . or herself? One of the pages in the address book had been ripped out. Could that page have contained the identity of her vicious vampire killer?

Two years before the Elizabeth Short killing, detectives discovered that Los Angeles did indeed have a twentieth-century Jack the Ripper in its midst – someone who had a taste for the blood of his victims.

On 15 November 1944, in the seedy downtown area of Los Angeles, in a run-down hotel at the corner of Fourth and Main streets, a maid discovered the mutilated body of a prostitute, Virginia Lee Griffin, sprawled on a bed. The street girl had been slashed open from her throat to her vagina and her entrails pulled out of her body. Her breasts had been cut off and an arm and a leg partly severed. The murder weapon, a razor-sharp carving knife, lay near the body.

Detectives began muttering they thought they had another Jack the Ripper on their hands. They became convinced when a second mutilation murder was reported in another downtown hotel only three blocks away. The victim was another prostitute, thirty-eight-year-old Lillian Johnson. Although she was not as severely mutilated as Virginia Griffin, the second victim had also been slashed from her throat to her thighs.

16

According to employees of both hotels each woman had checked in with someone. From all the descriptions it was definitely the same man. The tall and slender slayer with the black wavy hair, said all the witnesses, bore a striking resemblance to the then movie matinée idol Robert Taylor.

Armed with this invaluable information, that same evening police threw a dragnet around all the bars and hotels in the twenty-block downtown area.

Less than an hour into their bar-to-bar surveillance, a police officer spotted a man answering the suspect's description in a booth of a bar on Fourth Street – drinking wine and deep in conversation with a striking brunette in a tight red dress. The astute officer saw the man light a cigarette with a book of matches carrying the address of the hotel where Lillian Johnson had been found in the early hours of that day.

That was the clincher. Police moved in and arrested the good-looking stranger who identified himself as Otto Stephen Wilson, but who preferred to be called Steve.

It was pretty much an open-and-shut case. His finger-prints matched those at both crime scenes, and police had little difficulty in persuading Wilson to confess to both killings.

Police psychiatrist Dr Paul de Rover examined Wilson and declared him a normally placid guy who was over-whelmed by sadistic compulsions when he was under the influence of drink.

Wilson admitted to his bloodlust, telling police and doctors that his first wife had left him because of his bizarre compulsion to creep up on her when she was naked and slash at her buttocks with a razor. Wilson explained he liked nothing better than to kiss and lick the blood away as he cried and apologized for his weird behaviour.

These blood-lapping fantasies had got out of control when he picked up prostitute Virginia Griffin and later Lillian Johnson. Wilson confessed he was stalking a third victim when he was arrested.

With such violent sadistic tendencies, Wilson would have been a number one suspect in the Elizabeth Short slaying, but he was no longer around when the Black Dahlia succumbed to another blood-thirsty predator in January 1947. In September 1946, Steve Wilson – the Ripper who seemed to just sit around his crime scenes waiting to be arrested – was executed in the gas chamber of San Quentin prison.

Declining all last requests, Wilson's final words were, 'I've caused enough trouble for people already. I'll be better off out of the way.'

Four months later, detectives were wishing the killer of Elizabeth Short had felt the same way. Instead, the mystery of the Black Dahlia is still in the unsolved files. Could the vampire killer of the Black Dahlia still be walking among us?

RICHARD COTTINGHAM

He liked
to bite deep

Times Square, Manhattan, 1977 Someone was slaughtering hookers again, and this butcher had a viciousness all his own. Here was a sick murderer horrifying even the most hardened whores and pimps of that tough, bright, ugly district. It wasn't the number Mr Cottingham killed that mattered but, rather, the sheer perverted ferocity he demonstrated.

It was while putting out a blaze in a seedy 42nd Street hotel in December 1979 that firemen made the first revolting discovery of the work of Rich The Ripper. Trying to save a nude young woman he believed had been overcome by smoke, the first fireman in dragged the body out of the burning room into the hall. As he bent down over her to attempt mouth-to-mouth resuscitation, he found she had no head. The hands had been cut off as well, it turned out.

Later, a second naked body was discovered in the room, also headless and handless. It appeared that lighter fluid had been poured between their legs while they lay in bed and ignited. The buttocks and thighs had been badly seared. The missing parts of them were never found.

One of the victims was identified by X-rays as a twenty-two-year-old Long Island girl, Deedah Goodarzi, who had a record for prostitution. No one ever had a clue as to the identity of the other girl.

There was a new tension in the neighbourhood as the media poured in, interviewing pimps and hustlers and all manner of small-timers on the street. Most of the local people sensed a link between these recent killings and the slaughter, the year before, of a teenage runaway from the West Coast, called 'Bouncey'. She'd worked the streets not far from the hotel where the two headless girls had turned up. What was left of her had been discovered on a street in Queens. Bouncey had been cut up somewhere else and then her legs were dumped on one block, her body on another, and, yes, no head was found. The head had been severed just as in the more recent cases.

When detectives in both boroughs got together on the case they found significant points in common: all the victims were prostitutes, all were white and aged between eighteen and twenty-two, and all had probably worked the Times Square district. There was evidence in each case of torture inflicted prior to death. Inevitably, the killer was given the nickname 'Ripper' by the press.

Then months passed and nothing happened until May 1979 when a beautiful older streetwalker was found in a hotel room a few blocks downtown from Times Square, burned and cut with (this time) both breasts neatly, not violently, sliced off.

Meanwhile, a week or two before, unknown at first to the New York cops, a teenage prostitute called Shelly Dudley had been murdered in a motel room just over the George Washington Bridge in New Jersey. She had, apparently, been picked up in New York and driven to her doom.

The killer was in overdrive now and bound to get careless or at least, some cops believed, unlucky. The truth is that most crimes committed against strangers are solved 'statistically' because the perpetrator repeats himself too often. Rich the Ripper was about to become a statistic.

The reason truth is stranger than fiction is that in fiction you can't afford to be too stupid and absurd; in life there is no such limit. The killer, a little over two weeks later, brought a pretty young whore back to the *same* New Jersey motel where he'd murdered Shelly! He must have felt at home there.

On a bright May morning, about nine o'clock, the police arrived at the motel in response to a report of a woman screaming in a unit. People were in the parking lot pointing at the room. The cop went in around the back with a gun ready and met Mr Cottingham himself coming out with a pistol drawn. But Richard's gun turned out to be a replica with a sealed barrel and the only actual weapon he had was a knife.

In the room, the girl was in handcuffs, naked and badly hurt. She'd recently arrived in New York from Los Angeles, was 'turned out' by a pimp and had met this trick who'd spent a lot of money on her and brought her there. She'd only been on the street for a week and had been easily convinced that this man was going to save her from the life. He was being really sweet, she told police, until they got into the place; the next thing she knew he'd handcuffed her, slashed her with a knife, bit and ripped her body and licked her blood (as it seems he had with the others, qualifying him for vampiric status), whipped her, and continually raped and sodomized her. These tortures, with variations, went on for hours. At one point she said she got hold of his pistol for a moment. She tried to shoot him but thought the gun jammed. As he then increased the tempo of his torture the young girl went wild with panic and pain and started screaming – which saved her life because the maid called the police.

The similarities between this and the previous case at the same motel was not lost on the local detectives: especially the biting. The dead woman's right nipple was almost completely torn from her breast by his teeth. She had been handcuffed but with her mouth taped shut. He must have forgotten the tape with his latest victim.

The man they apprehended was a pretty unlikely suspect, at first glance. He was Richard Cottingham, a near-sighted, thirty-three-year-old father of three who lived in Lodi, New Jersey, and was well respected in the nice, middle-class neighbourhood. He was a computer operator with Blue Cross/Blue Shield and had put in a competent thirteen years of service, according to his superiors.

His first problem (apart from the living victim herself)

was the briefcase he'd been caught with: it was packed with items essential to any computer operator, such as three sets of handcuffs, a bondage gag, slave collars and so forth!

A search of his private 'trophy room' at home turned up lots of items belonging to various victims, including clothes, purses, etc. It seems that his wife had just filed for divorce and they hadn't had sexual relations for years. Court records revealed he'd been arrested in the past for prostitution-related offences but the cases had been dismissed.

There had been, police discovered, at least three other women (two prostitutes and a housewife) who'd been tortured and raped in his usual style, including bloodletting and sucking blood from torn breasts. The housewife had been pregnant. She'd been enticed into his car from a bar, been attacked, and then had her breasts burned with a cigarette lighter before being tossed from the moving vehicle.

Cottingham periodically attempted suicide after his capture, making headlines when he leaped to his feet in court, slipped a razor blade from under the bandage he was wearing on his wrist from a previous attempt, then screamed that he was innocent while slashing his other wrist. Despite these histrionics, he was convicted and sentenced to hundreds of years in jail for dozens of crimes, including multiple murders.

WAYNE BODEN

Canada's vampire
rapist

In 1968 when the police found the strangled body of twenty-one-year-old schoolteacher Norma Vaillancourt in her Montreal apartment, they were surprised to see a relaxed, somehow serene, pleased look on her face despite the fact that she had been violently raped, her breasts torn and pitted with vicious bite marks and strangled. She had a number of boyfriends all of whom were cleared in the subsequent investigation.

The following year another victim, Shirley Audette, was found on an apartment patio in the same city, fully clothed but none the less raped and strangled with apparently matching teethmarks on her breasts. It seemed obvious the killer was no stranger because, again, there was no evidence of resistance, no bloody skin under the nails (common in attack cases), for example. Tests showed the victims hadn't been drugged and weren't drunk at the time of death. It seemed almost as if, some imaginative detective thought, both women had been put under a spell. This killer was a lover as well as a Dracula who sucked a little blood instead of milk from women's breasts.

One of Audette's boyfriends told the police that he believed she had got involved with a very dominant, attractive man because the girl had said, with both fear and a thrill, apparently, that she was scared and getting into 'something dangerous'. The killer seemed to have an eye for girls who accepted what today is termed 'rough sex'.

It was now November 1969. The next luckless woman, Marielle Archambault, a jewellery salesgirl in a Mont-real shop, was met at closing time by a well-dressed young man she introduced as 'Bill'. After he had left with her some co-workers remarked she seemed really happy and entranced by the fellow.

Needless to say, she didn't show up at work the next day. Her landlady was called and went to see if she were ill. Marielle was on the living-room floor under a blanket. This time the spell hadn't worked because there were signs she had put up a terrific struggle before she died. The killer had ripped off her tights and bra, raped her, and had done his loathsome biting on her breasts.

The cops found a crumpled photograph which turned out to be of the man called 'Bill' who'd taken her home the previous night. A police sketch from the picture published in the newspapers drew no response.

'Bill' waited two months and then hooked up with twenty-four-year-old Jean Way. In January 1970 Jean's boyfriend came to pick her up. When she didn't answer the door he left for a while and came back a little later.

26

This time the door was unlocked and she was lying nude on the sofa with the trademark savagely bitten breasts. It looked as if the vampire had been in the house when the other man had knocked at 8.15 p.m. The murderer's charm, or his powers of hypnosis, was back on track because, once again, there had been no struggle and there was a somehow pleased look on the dead girl's face.

By now there was massive publicity, and 'Bill' was on Canada's 'most wanted' list. However deranged, on balance 'Bill' wasn't stupid. He travelled 2,500 miles to Calgary, where, in May 1971, he found Elizabeth Anne Porteous, a high-school teacher. She, too, failed to report for work one morning. For the second time he'd made an imperfect choice of woman because there was a desperate fight with the usual outcome – only, this time, there was a broken cufflink under the raped and mutilated body.

It turned out Elizabeth had been seen by two fellow teachers the night before stopped at traffic lights in a blue Mercedes. The car had some kind of beef advertisement sticker on the rear window. Also, others knew she'd recently been dating a man named 'Bill'. They painted a picture of a 'flashy' dresser with neat, short hair. That was the right description too.

The vehicle was spotted soon after in the same neighbourhood and when Wayne Clifford Boden went to his car the Mounties got their man. He admitted dating Elizabeth and said the cufflink was his, but claimed she was fine when he left her that night. Still, there was the photograph and he looked like the photograph.

27

Ironically, it was a dentist who nailed the coffin shut on the vampire. The jury was convinced by the 'tooth-prints'. Boden began confessing after that and collected a whole string of life sentences.

One thing was learned: Boden didn't set out to kill anybody. It was while making love and, with a certain degree of consent, semi-strangling his partners, that he freaked out with an overpowering need to rip and suck their bared breasts. Feasting himself, he gripped the girls into an unstruggling unconsciousness and held on until they died.

MARCELO DE ANDRADE

Mummy's boy drank victims' blood to make himself more handsome

Rio de Janeiro, Brazil   Twenty-five-year-old mummy's boy Marcelo de Andrade worshipped his mother, and went to church four times a week, but over a nine-month period in 1991, he still found time as a vampire killer to kill, sodomize, and drink the blood of fourteen young boys aged from six to thirteen. And the reason he drank their blood and feasted on their flesh, the demented Rio homosexual told police, was because he would 'become beautiful just like them'.

The disappearance of Rio's street urchins has long been a problem in the bustling Brazilian metropolis. Most are the victims of warped vigilantes trying to 'clean up' the streets. De Andrade's mission was more evil and sinister.

His killings ended when he 'fell in love' with ten-year-old Altair de Abreu, who told police a gruesome tale of watching the killing and sodomy of his six-year-old brother. Altair told Rio murder investigator Inspector Romeu José Vieira: 'A man called Marcelo came up to me and my brother Ivan at a bus station and said he would give us money if we helped him light candles to a saint.

'We were heading for a church, but as we crossed a vacant lot, Marcelo suddenly turned on Ivan and started strangling him. I was so paralysed by fear I could not run away. I watched in horror, tears streaming down my cheeks, as he killed and then raped my brother. When he was finished with Ivan, he turned to me, hugged me, and said he loved me.'

After agreeing to spend the night with de Andrade, little Altair managed to run away and went straight to the police with his terrifying story.

'Falling in love with Altair was de Andrade's big mistake – he let him live,' said Inspector Vieira after de Andrade's arrest and confession. 'When we arrived at the place where de Andrade lived, he was very calm. He quickly confessed to Ivan's murder – but it took two months of questioning before he admitted to the others.

'He appeared very fragile and delicate. It was blood-chilling to hear him talk of these horrors in his quiet, soft voice. De Andrade told me, "I preferred young boys because they are better looking and have soft skin. And the priest said that children automatically go to heaven if they die before they're thirteen. So I know I did them a favour by sending them to heaven." '

De Andrade confessed that he loved to cut off his victims' heads with a machete he borrowed from his doting mother, then drink the spurting blood.

Still under psychiatric evaluation, de Andrade awaits trial in Rio.

THE VAMPIRE PERVERT

ALBERT FISH

Gentle grandad was really the king of perverted vampire monsters

He looked like every kid's favourite grandfather, but behind the gentle façade of the silver hair and moustache and watery blue eyes lurked a blood-lusting monster who preyed on small children.

Crime historians are still arguing over exactly how many kids fell victim to Albert Howard Fish, certainly one of the most perverted sex killers in the annals of US crime history. What's pretty certain is that there were dozens of murder victims, and hundreds of molested children in a quarter of a century.

Vampirism, cannibalism, dismemberment and every sado-masochistic perversion known to man were all part of the murderous repertoire of Albert Fish who, prematurely decrepit at the age of sixty-six, was and still is one of the oldest men ever put to death in the electric chair.

Polite, well-mannered, and devoutly religious, Fish was the unlikeliest of predators. That's why he had no difficulty persuading the parents of twelve-year-old

Grace Budd to let the child accompany him to a birthday party on Sunday, 3 June 1928. They had no idea they had entrusted their child to a monster.

The kidnapping of Grace Budd is as good a place as any to start recounting the horrible saga of Albert Fish. Her abduction led to a manhunt which lasted six years. Police had given up hope of ever solving her mysterious disappearance when a slender clue – gleaned from a mean-spirited anonymous letter written to the missing girl's parents – led dogged detectives to Fish, his arrest, and the revelations of his gruesome life story of murder and perversion.

Fish introduced himself to the Budd family in an innocuous way. They were far from well off. The father, Albert, earned a modest living as a doorman, but hardly enough to care for his family of five, which included wife Delia, eighteen-year-old Edward, Albert Jr, Grace and five-year-old Beatrice. To try to help the family out, the able-bodied eldest son Edward put an advertisement in the 27 May 1928 issue of the New York *World Telegram*: 'Young man, 18, wishes position in the country', followed by his name and address.

That same day, at 3.30 in the afternoon, dapperly dressed Fish came knocking on the Budds' door at 406 West 15th Street in the Chelsea district of Manhattan, in answer to the *World Telegram* ad. He introduced himself as Mr Frank Howard, a farmer from Farmingdale, Long Island, who was willing to pay $15 per week to a willing young worker. Well-paying jobs for young men were hard to come by back in those days, and the Budd family could scarcely believe young Eddie's good fortune. Mr

Howard was welcomed into the house.

After he had described his farm and outlined his proposition to hire Edward as a live-in farm hand, Edward readily accepted the job. The old gentleman even suggested there might be a position for Eddie's best friend and neighbour, Willie. He agreed to return the following week and drive them both to Farmingdale.

Because of that promise the Budds were somewhat disappointed when the gentlemanly Mr Howard did not return on the appointed day, Saturday, 2 June. He did, however, send a polite telegram of apology – and he did show up at their door the following day.

This time, impressed by his manners and solicitous nature, the Budds greeted him like a long-lost friend of the family. They invited him to stay for lunch. He behaved exactly like a visiting grandfather. There was a twinkle in the old man's eye when, after lunch, he took a wad of dollar bills out of his pocket and peeled off two which he presented to Eddie and Willie. He told the youths that he had a prior engagement, but that they should go to a film. He would pick them up to take them to the farm that evening.

He had a special treat in store for their daughter Grace, he told her trusting parents. If they were agreeable, he wanted to take her to a children's birthday party at the home of his married sister at 137th Street and Columbus Avenue in New York City.

The Budds readily agreed. Their equally trusting daughter, still wearing the new virginal white Communion dress she had worn to church that morning, clapped her hands with glee. Grace could scarcely stand still from excitement as her mother dressed her in her best spring coat with fur-trimmed collar and cuffs. She also wore a little grey hat with blue streamers, and carried a small brown leather bag. She made a pretty picture – a perfect little girl off to enjoy herself at a Sunday afternoon birthday party.

Her parents waved goodbye happily as their dark-eyed twelve-year-old daughter skipped down the street hand in hand with her grandfather from hell.

She did not return that night. The party must have run late . . . She's probably staying overnight with Mr Howard's sister . . . The anxious Budds tried to convince themselves. The following morning there was still no Grace.

A worried Albert Budd scurried to check the address at 137th and Columbus – only to find it did not exist. Columbus only went as far north as 109th.

His next step was to go to the police, where he was immediately referred to veteran detective Will King of the Missing Persons Bureau. Detective King smelled a rat from the start. It didn't take him long to discover there was no Frank Howard with a farm in Farmingdale. Nor was there any clue to the abductor's identity. The crafty old pervert had covered his tracks impeccably – even retrieving the telegram he had sent the Budds claiming that he was going to complain to Western Union, because it was incorrectly addressed.

Detective King nevertheless instigated a long and arduous official search for the Western Union copy of the telegram Mr Howard had sent the Budds. After all, it was the only slender existing thread which might lead to the kidnapper's true identity. Three postal clerks spent a total of fifteen hours sifting through tens of thousands of telegram duplicates before they found the one they were looking for. All it told the investigators was that it had been sent from the East Harlem office of Western Union.

But what to do now? Search every home in East Harlem? That idea was considered, then abandoned as a physically impossible task.

Detective King clutched at another straw – some cheese and a carton of fresh strawberries which the old stranger had brought Mrs Budd as a gift. He had told Mrs Budd these were fresh products from his farm.

On a hunch, investigators scoured the East Harlem area until they found the delicatessen where he had bought the cheese, and a street vendor who remembered selling him the strawberries. The peddler was able to describe 'Mr Howard' to a tee, but he could recall nothing else significant about his customer. That trail too ran cold.

Grace Budd's disappearance provoked a widespread hue and cry in New York City that autumn, particularly when the detectives and family told their story to the media. Little Grace's likeness was emblazoned over all the front pages and gave rise to hundreds of tips and pieces of advice from an angry public.

One lead that looked promising was a woman who called the police to reveal that she had an uncle called Frank Howard who once farmed in Farmingdale, Long Island. But that angle fizzled out completely when the woman announced that that Frank Howard had closed his farm in Farmingdale a long time ago and moved to Chicago – where he had died ten years earlier!

One thousand circulars with a description and picture of Grace, and a description of her abductor Howard were printed and circulated to police forces throughout the United States and Canada – with no results. The Budds' hearts sank as lead after lead got nowhere.

A couple of months after Grace's disappearance even the most tenacious of the investigators – with the exception of Detective Will King – had just about given the case up as hopeless.

Detective King, already a legend among New York's finest for his tenacity and determination, was the only law enforcement investigator who never gave up hope. Not a day went by that he didn't think of poor Grace and her distraught parents. He followed up every lead that crossed his desk. King was sure he was on to his man when he received a dossier on a glib, grey-haired con artist and forger called Albert Corthell, who was on the run for trying to abduct a little girl from an adoption agency.

For months Will King tracked down Corthell, chasing him from city to city, travelling a total of 40,000 miles criss-crossing the country on his crusade. He was crushed when he finally ran Corthell to earth only to discover he had a perfect alibi – he had been in prison in Seattle, Washington, the other side of the country, when young Grace was abducted.

Corthell was one of only two really hot leads over a period of six long years. The other strong suspect, Charles Edward Pope, was also arrested and actually charged with little Grace's kidnapping. But the principal witness, Mrs Budd, admitted at his trial that she had mistakenly picked out the wrong man. It turned out that Pope had been fingered for the kidnapping by a vindictive ex-wife and he was subsequently released.

Around the same time that Corthell and Pope were the subject of exhaustive police inquiries, another grey-haired old man, whose name was Fish, was arrested in New York City and charged with sending obscene materials, namely letters, through the mail. The letters were to a well-known Hollywood movie producer and in them Fish offered him large sums of money if he could put Fish in touch with women prepared to indulge in sado-masochistic orgies with him. He was committed to the psychiatric ward at Bellevue Hospital for a ten-day observation.

The withered and frail-looking obscene-letter writer claimed that, although his friends knew him as Albert, his real name was Hamilton Fish, and he was related to the famous New York family of the same name. (He was to give the same story when he was again arrested four years later, this time for the atrocious murder of Grace Budd – and there's never been any reason to doubt that he hailed from prestigious family stock.)

Fish in fact stayed in Bellevue for nearer thirty days that winter of 1930. He was polite, co-operative, and doctors judged him sane. They did diagnose him as having various sexual hang-ups, but they attributed that to dementia associated with advancing years. He was judged harmless, and released from Bellevue on probation into the custody of his daughter Anna.

As the years rolled by, apart from Detective King's sterling, unstinting efforts, the Grace Budd case was otherwise shelved.

Then, on 11 November 1934 – six years after the kidnapping – out of the blue Mrs Budd received an anonymous letter. The letter claimed to have been written by a friend of someone called Captain John Davis. Captain Davis, said the anonymous friend, was a seafaring man who, in one of his trips to China, developed a taste for human flesh, particularly the flesh of children which Captain Davis had eaten during a famine in the orient.

The unsigned letter got even more bizarre. It described in graphic terms how Captain Davis, on his return to New York, had kidnapped and murdered two small boys, cooked their flesh and eaten it. Obviously the outpourings of a deranged mind, the letter stated that Captain Davis had told the writer that the flesh of children was 'good and tender'. With that in mind, he had decided to try it for himself – and he could not resist the urge the day he visited the Budds' home for lunch and young Grace sat on his knee.

An anguished Mrs Budd sobbed hysterically as the writer proceeded to detail how he had taken young Grace to an empty house in Westchester, New York, where he let her pick flowers in the garden while he went into the house and stripped naked.

He called her indoors, where she burst out crying when she saw the naked and grizzled old demon. She tried to run away, but he caught her, stripped her, and choked her to death. Then he dismembered the child's body into small pieces which he cooked and ate.

'How sweet her tender little arse was, roasted in the oven,' he said in his gruesome confession letter. 'It took me nine days to eat her entire body. I did not fuck her though I could have, had I wished. She died a virgin.'

After this horrifying letter, investigators again sprang into action, pulling out all the stops to find the monstrous perpetrator. Fastest into action was Detective Will King, who had even deferred his retirement two years earlier so he could continue to work on the Grace Budd case.

Will King immediately dug out the duplicate of 'Mr Howard's' original telegram. There was no doubt about it. The handwriting was the same. 'Howard' and this latter-day letter writer were one and the same.

Under a microscope, Detective King discovered an almost indiscernible design on the flap of the envelope, which became legible when placed under the more powerful spectroscope. It turned out to be the letters NYPCBA. A quick flick through the Manhattan telephone directory revealed these letters to stand for the New York Private Chauffeurs Benevolent Association, headquartered at 627 Lexington Avenue.

The association gladly opened their doors and their files to Detective King, who spent hours checking the background and handwriting of the association's employees – all 400 of them. Sadly, he could not come up with a match.

Undaunted, Detective King called all the employees together, and put them through rigorous questioning. Did anyone know anything which would be helpful in the

Budd case? Did any of them ever take association stationery home for their personal use? If anyone had any information along these lines, appealed the investigator, then they would be given immunity for any theft that might be involved. All the police were interested in was catching a sadistic and deranged child killer before he struck again.

After his appeal, Will King sat in a private office at the association's headquarters and prayed for some kind of response. It came in the form of a nondescript little man in a chauffeur's uniform called Lee Sicowski, who knocked on the door, sat down timidly and announced to Detective King that he was in the habit of taking the association's stationery home with him and using it. In fact, said Sicowski, he had left some notepaper and envelopes unused in a room he had occupied at 622 Lexington. Detectives raced to the rooming house, but there were no envelopes or notepaper in Sicowski's old room. Was this to be another dead end?

'Think again,' Detective King urged Sicowski. 'Where else could the stationery be?' Sicowski then remembered he had spent some time in a cheap boarding house at 200 East 52nd Street – maybe he had left stationery there.

The East 52nd Street address proved to be a cheap flophouse. But the investigators struck gold. The landlady, Mrs Frieda Schneider, said that yes, indeed, there was a man living there who answered Frank Howard's description. In fact, he was still there – Mr Albert Fish, living in room number seven. Carefully, Detective King checked the signature in the flophouse register – A.H.

Smith. It was the same handwriting. He had found his man!

Will King's heart sank when the landlady told him that Fish had checked out. But he was expected back, she hastily added encouragingly. He was in the habit of getting a monthly cheque from one of his sons. And his mail was always addressed to 200 East 52nd.

Detective King was prepared to invest a few more weeks, months if necessary, waiting for Fish. After all, he had been on his tail for six long years. Detective King took a room in the flophouse at the top of the stairs, giving him a commanding view of both the entrance and the upstairs and downstairs hallways.

He was to wait over three weeks before he struck gold again. On 13 December 1934, Detective King had gone to attend to paperwork at police headquarters when he got an urgent call from the flophouse: Fish was back.

When he returned to East 52nd Street, landlady Schneider was waiting for him at the door. Fish had come back half an hour earlier, she whispered. He normally didn't stay as long as this – she was afraid he was going to leave again any time. She had given him a cup of tea in one of the furnished rooms.

Forcing himself to stay calm, Detective King quickly checked his .38 police issue revolver, went to the room and knocked on the door. What confronted him was a harmless-looking, white-haired old man with a straggly grey moustache and watery blue eyes, slurping a cup of tea.

Detective King identified himself; Fish did not attempt to deny his own identity. Then the officer asked

Fish if he would accompany him to police headquarters for questioning. Will King got the shock of his life. Without warning, this seemingly, harmless old creature reached into his pocket and lunged at King, brandishing a vicious razor blade. Fish, fortunately, was no match for the solidly built cop. Will King grabbed Fish by the wrist and twisted his hand until the razor blade went flying.

Detective King handcuffed his aged prisoner. Then he frisked him – to his horror, Fish's pockets were crammed full of assorted sharp knives and razor blades!

'I've got you now,' Detective King told Fish triumphantly.

At the police station, Fish seemed more resigned to his arrest and disclosure as the kidnapper-killer of Grace Budd. The blood thirst had come over him that summer of 1928, and it had been necessary for him to select a victim.

Yes, he said, he was the stranger who called on the Budds that summer. He explained that at first he had meant his victim to be Edward Budd, the older son who had advertised for a job. But when he got to the house and saw the size of stocky teenager Edward, he abandoned his desire for a male sacrifice and turned his sights on the more vulnerable Grace. He freely confessed to abducting innocent Grace, taking her by train to a dilapidated building, Wisteria Cottage, in a place called Worthington Woods, in Westchester County on the outskirts of New York city.

Fish's memory of Grace Budd's last day on earth was remarkably clear after six years. He remembered that he had bought a round-trip ticket to Worthington for himself – and a one-way ticket for little Grace.

He also remembered that when they were changing trains he had left a bundle behind on one train. Grace, to be helpful, ran back to retrieve it for him. Inside the bundle were the tools of Fish's grisly trade – a saw, a cleaver and a butcher's knife. The little girl obligingly handed over to Fish the devil's tools that were to be used on her a short while later. Fish, in fact, liked to call the tools of his evil trade his 'implements of hell'.

As he outlined in his letter, it was at Wisteria Cottage – an abandoned house where he had himself lived years ago – that he coldly and systematically strangled her, beheaded, mutilated and dismembered her body, dissected her torso at the waist and then proceeded to eat her over a nine-day period.

Fish particularly relished recounting how he had cut off his victim's head, holding her over a five-gallon paint drum so as not to lose as much as a drop of her precious, warm blood. His eyes rolled in his head as he told how he drank his young victim's blood – gulping down so much that he even made himself sick.

His interrogators were incredulous. They could hardly believe the horror spouting from the mouth of this refined old grandfather.

A trip to the scene of the crime recovered the grisly skeletal remains of Grace Budd, buried in pieces beside a stone wall at the rear of Wisteria Cottage.

And Fish couldn't stop confessing. He ended up confessing to 400 child murders, committed between 1910 when he was forty years old, and 1934. Much of what he told police later turned out to be false or exaggerated, but he still provided enough details of his gory past to chill the hardened detectives. Given his insatiable sexual appetite and obvious bloodlust, the investigators were left in no doubt that his victims must have amounted to well over 100 poor souls.

When asked by reporters pointblank about other unsolved child killings and disappearances, all Fish would say was: 'Well boys, you might as well accuse me of all of them. You can't do me any more damage.'

When the newspapers hit the stands, Fish was described in headlines in such colourful prose as 'Vampire Man', the 'Aged Thrill-Killer', the 'Werewolf of Wisteria' and the 'Orgiastic Fiend'.

Digging out police dossiers on Fish, the detectives weren't really surprised to find out he had a long criminal record going way back to 1903 when he'd served sixteen months in Sing Sing on a grand larceny charge. But what really chilled and frustrated investigators was the fact that Fish had been arrested in the New York area *six* times since the disappearance of Grace Budd, on charges ranging from petty larceny, to vagrancy, to sending obscene literature through the post. Three of the arrests took place in the three-month period immediately after Grace's kidnapping – and each time the charges against him were dismissed. As for the others, he walked free each time after either a short period of detention, or with a legal slap on the wrist. No one had ever thought of him as a diseased and depraved killer.

One of the few people not surprised at the arrest of Fish was his son and one-time roommate, Albert Fish Jr. 'That old skunk . . . I always knew he'd get caught for something like this,' said Fish Jr, who went on to explain how he had returned unexpectedly to their apartment one day and had found his sick father stripped naked and flagellating himself with heavy boards studded with sharp nails.

When the moon was full, revealed Fish Jr, his old man greedily used to demand raw steak for dinner. Concluded Albert Fish Jr disgustedly: 'I've never wanted anything to do with him, and I'll not lift a hand to help him.'

New York tabloid writers had a field day with the younger Fish's disclosure that his dad liked raw steak during full moon periods. This remark was given even more weight when weather bureau records for 3 June 1928, the date Grace Budd disappeared, showed that the moon was at its fullest. Naturally, this led to a new tabloid nickname for the old ghoul – 'The Moon Maniac'.

A number of psychiatrists examined Fish and found the soft-spoken patriarch – estranged from his wife, but father of three sons and three daughters, grandfather of eight – to be a psychopath.

If he was to be likened to anyone, said one psychiatrist, it would be to the German monster Fritz Haarmann, the notorious Vampire of Hanover, who lived a life of unspeakable depravity, killing young boys then selling their flesh as steak at a local meat market. It wasn't surprising then that when police went through Fish's personal belongings they found hundreds of newspaper clippings on the depraved activities of Fritz Haarmann.

Albert Fish was way up there with the all-time killer monsters. He not only relished his notoriety, he enjoyed describing to teams of fascinated doctors his fetishes and perversions – such as inserting needles into his scrotum (X-rays revealed twenty-seven rusting needles), and inserting cotton wool doused with lighter fluid in his anus and setting it alight.

One psychiatrist in particular, Dr Frederic Wertham, got remarkably close to Fish before and after his trial. Their relationship was much like Professor Karl Berg, the analyst, had with the Vampire of Düsseldorf, the depraved killer Peter Kurten.

In his book *The Show of Violence*, Dr Wertham revealed that Fish impressed him greatly as a one-of-a-kind psychopath. 'Fish looked like a meek and innocuous little old man, gentle and benevolent, friendly and polite,' wrote the good doctor. 'If you wanted someone to entrust your children to, he would be the one you would choose.' Dr Wertham went on to describe Fish as the most complex example of 'a polymorphous pervert' he had ever known – someone who had practised almost every perversion known to man: every sexual deviation from sodomy to sadism to eating excrement and self-mutilation.

It was only to Dr Wertham that Fish confided that he had drunk Grace Budd's still-warm blood, but had gagged on it after taking three or four deep quaffs. And it was to Dr Wertham that the Vampire of Wisteria Cottage disclosed how he had cut off Grace Budd's ears and nose, wrapping them with other fleshy parts of her body in an old newspaper.

Fish related how he sat during the train journey back into New York on the day of the killing, with the newspaper bundle on his lap, quivering with sexual excitement just by holding the body parts of the unfortunate twelve-year-old close to him.

Like other examining physicians, Dr Wertham pronounced Fish insane. Dr Wertham told the court: 'I can tell you that, to the best of my medical knowledge, every sexual abnormality that I have ever heard of this man has practised – not only has he thought about it, not only has he daydreamed about it, but he has practised it. Fish is a sadist of incredible cruelty.' The psychiatrist added that Fish was also a homosexual, a paedophile with a penchant for children aged between five to fourteen years, and a deviant with no fewer than seventeen perversions that he practised on a regular basis.

As a self-employed painter, said Dr Wertham, Fish had skulked around basements and cellars for fifty years stalking and preying on innocent young children in as many as twenty-three states. 'There were so many instances that I can't begin to tell you exactly how many there were. But I believe to the best of my knowledge that he has raped one hundred children. At least,' said the doctor.

Fish's defence counsel, attorney James Dempsey, alluding to the needles and the nail-studded paddles, told the trial jury that they were dealing with a tragic mental case. 'We do not have to prove he is insane,' Dempsey told the jury. 'Rather it is up to the State to prove that he is sane.'

Defence attorney Dempsey had only one question for Dr Wertham, lead psychiatrist for the defence – but that one question was about Fish's sanity and it took one hour and fifteen minutes for Dempsey to read it as it was, 15,000 words long, covering forty-five typewritten pages. Dr Wertham needed only three words to reply: 'He is insane.'

The jury, however, were convinced of Fish's sanity – at least in the courtroom they were – and sentenced him to die in the chair. Ironically, a snap poll of jurors after the trial revealed that the majority of them in fact agreed with attorney Dempsey and Dr Wertham that Fish was indeed a stark, raving lunatic. But because his crimes were so downright heinous they felt it only right that he should be electrocuted anyway.

On being found guilty, Fish's initial response was flip: 'Going to the electric chair will be the supreme thrill of my life.'

However, as his appointment with the executioner grew closer, Fish was seen to be spending a lot of time on his knees in his cell, praying that somehow he would be spared the ultimate penalty. He even coughed up a few more full and frank confessions to other gruesome killings and related how he had drunk the blood of other children he had murdered, with the hint that he might confess to more . . . if the death sentence was over-turned.

On 16 January 1936, Albert Fish ate his last meal on death row at Sing Sing – a T-bone steak from which the bone had been carefully removed in case he tried to use it to cheat the executioner. His final words as he was being led to the electrocution chamber were: 'I don't know why I'm here.'

To this day, there exists an apocryphal story about the Fish execution. Legend has it that the metal needles in the old man's body almost short-circuited the electric chair, erupting in a bright spray of blue sparks. It isn't true. There was no light show. Albert Fish, monster extraordinary, died like an ordinary man.

FRITZ HAARMANN

Fiendish vampire of Hanover
sold victims' flesh as steaks

In the perverted tradition of vampire-cannibal Albert
Fish and the fiendish Peter Kurten, petty-criminal-
turned-vampire Fritz Haarmann has earned himself a
special niche in the annals of twentieth-century vampires. Dubbed the 'Vampire of Hanover' because of
his perverted thirst for blood, Haarmann was also a
cannibal – who even turned a pretty profit selling his
victims' flesh as steaks in impoverished, war-ravaged
Germany.

Born in 1879, the sixth child of a poor family and
mildly retarded, the epileptic bisexual Haarmann
revealed perverse tendencies at an early age. As a
pre-teen, he loved to dress up as a girl. He openly
expressed hatred for his bad-tempered father, a stoker
on a train.

Arrested for child molesting when he was seventeen,
he was declared 'incurably feeble-minded' by a psychiatrist and committed to an asylum at Hildesheim for six

months. Spurning treatment, he escaped and went to Switzerland, before making his way home again to Hanover. He made a brief attempt to settle down, becoming engaged to a young local girl he made pregnant. The baby was stillborn. Haarmann called the wedding off, and ran away again – this time to join the army, where he actually won praise from his superiors as 'a born soldier'. Things might have been different for him if he had remained in the army where he appeared to be in his element. But he was diagnosed as having neurasthenia and given a medical discharge.

In 1903 back in civvy street, Haarmann embarked on a life of petty, and not so petty, crime. He indulged in such offences as theft, fraud, burglary and indecency but wasn't even a clever criminal, so he spent most of his twenties in and out of jail. In fact, the once model soldier sat out the First World War behind bars.

After the war, he turned to child molesting again, and did another nine-month stint in jail for an offence against a young boy.

On his release, he moved to Hanover's unsavoury Old Quarter and got into cahoots with a good-looking young male prostitute called Hans Grans. They made a sleazy twosome, preying ruthlessly on the young male war refugees that flooded into the city looking for somewhere to stay.

Police records show that Haarmann and Grans were responsible for the killings of at least twenty-seven young refugees – but Haarmann's official personal kill tally is estimated at closer to fifty. So, although Haarmann was accused of the disappearance of only twenty-seven, police closed their missing person files on a total of fifty cases.

Unofficially, the police believed the head count might be much higher. Between the years of 1918 and 1923, in the Hanover area approximately 600 young boys, aged between fifteen and eighteen, were reported missing. Haarmann could have been responsible for many of those disappearances.

His *modus operandi* was always the same. With the promise of good beer and a hearty meal he would lure likely young prospects, seeking the comforts of a home, to his rooming-house at Cellarstrasse 27. There – often with his friend Grans looking on – Haarmann turned into a true vampire. After a hearty dinner and several steins of strong beer, his young prey would become sleepy and helpless.

Depraved and out of control, Haarmann would leap on his victim, sinking his teeth like an animal's fangs into a defenceless young lad's throat. Haarmann would hang on to the throat tenaciously, ripping flesh and slurping warm blood until the victim expired. Death invariably occurred after Haarmann severed the windpipe. In many cases, the victims' heads were almost severed from their bodies – by the sheer ferocity and sharpness of Haarmann's teeth.

One of the first victims was a young seventeen-year-old called Friedel Rothe whom Haarmann and Grans accosted and invited to Cellarstrasse 27 shortly after his arrival at the city's railway station. The hungry young lad went with them . . . never to be seen again.

Worried friends reported Rothe's disappearance to

police. In the course of their investigation, they paid a visit to convicted criminal Haarmann, who was also a paid police informer on the Hanover underworld. He invited the police in to his lodgings, but they could find no trace of the missing youth. What they didn't know was that young Rothe's severed head was wrapped in newspapers and hidden behind a stove in the squalid quarters.

A self-proclaimed butcher by trade, Haarmann made little effort to keep his night-time dismembering and carving activities quiet. Later, neighbours were to report that they frequently heard strange noises coming from Haarmann's rooms – 'like the sound of chopping'. At one time he even offered his landlady a bundle of bones to make soup. She politely declined the offer, telling police later: 'They looked too white to be good soup bones!'

Usually working together with Grans, Haarmann would butcher the bodies of their young victims, carving portions of the corpses into appetizing-looking steaks. Then they would take their devilish produce to the bustling Schieber open-air market, opposite Hanover's railway station, where they would sell the steak-size portions to unsuspecting shoppers out hunting for food bargains.

It was common knowledge in Hanover – which had become a crime-infested city of degenerates in the early 1920s – that Schieber market was the place to go if you were on the lookout for cheap black-market produce. With Hans Grans, Haarmann became known as a vendor of black-market meat.

Inedible portions of their victims, plus their meagre personal belongings, were dumped into the nearby Leine Canal.

Haarmann and Grans' butcher business went undetected for several years . . . until one discerning woman shopper became suspicious of her 'steaks'. Suspecting the meat might not be what the duo claimed it to be, she took a sample to Hanover police headquarters for analysis. Although one police lab technician declared the 'steaks' to be pork rather than red meat, detectives remained suspicious of the Haarmann–Grans enterprise, particularly because of the ever-increasing numbers of young boys being reported missing and their awareness of Haarmann's and Grans' kinky sex preferences.

It wasn't until May 1924, however, that the murder investigation swung into full gear. First, several skulls came ashore on the banks of the Leine Canal. Then a group of schoolboys found a sackful of human bones floating in the canal.

Faced with such evidence, the Hanover police called in psychological experts from Berlin. As they went through police files, Haarmann's name and record came up again and again as a likely suspect. It was time to pay him a visit, decided police.

At his rooming-house, they discovered bundle after bundle of clothing belonging to missing boys – clothes that Haarmann had greedily kept to sell instead of dropping into the canal. Haarmann broke down under interrogation and confessed. Like most of his kind do when flushed out, he began recounting with unconcealed excitement and relish all of his crimes. He happily put his signature to a grisly confession of his misdeeds.

Incredibly, a decade later and 4,000 miles away in the United States, a whole batch of clippings about Haarmann's depraved life were found in the possession of the vampire-grandfather, New Yorker Albert Fish – obviously a great fan of the Vampire of Hanover. Even Fish would have had a hard job keeping up with Haarmann's depravity which won him the following nicknames by crime chroniclers: 'The Chief Murderer', 'The Worst Man' and 'The Last of the Human Race'.

Obsessed with blood until the very end, Haarmann – found guilty at Hanover Assizes in December 1924 – made a stomach-churning plea to be put to death by decapitation, the goriest end he could dream up for himself. The disgusted authorities were happy to oblige and Haarmann's head was, at his own request, chopped off by a sword in the city marketplace. After the grisly public execution, his brain was removed from the skull for examination by forensic pathologists at Goettingen University.

His gullible accomplice Grans was jailed for life, later commuted to twelve years' imprisonment since Haarmann had owned up to being the prime instigator and actual killer.

PETER KURTEN

The Vampire of Düsseldorf:
'This is what love's about!'

If anyone ever earned the modern-day vampire label it was Peter Kurten, who roamed the streets of Düsseldorf, Germany, in the 1920s, sadistically preying on young women and children. Before he was caught, his predatory activities sent the entire city into a state of panic and terror – much like the notorious Jack the Ripper had done in the city of London a few decades earlier.

Forty-eight-year-old Kurten, like many of our other vampire killers, was an unlikely looking monster. Well-mannered, soft spoken and a natty dresser, he was a personable man. Children took to him easily. The ladies thought him a real charmer. He was the last person you would have imagined to be a psychopath. If anything, he would be labelled harmless. Yet his polite, bourgeois exterior masked the vile heart of one of the most brutal and sadistic vampire killers of all time.

Very much into sexual fantasies and lustful day-dreams, Kurten associated sexual satisfaction with blood-letting. As he stabbed and strangled his helpless victims, he would experience orgasm and tell them: 'This is what love's about.'

No one would have guessed he was already known to the police as a sociopath and misfit who had spent half his life in prisons for a variety of crimes, including sexual offences. For years, he carefully disguised the fact that he was also a murderous psychopath who revelled in thoughts of drawing blood from innocent victims. He committed his first murder as a young man in 1913. His victim was a helpless, ten-year-old girl.

After his belated arrest in 1930, he waxed nostalgic as he described that first killing seventeen years earlier. He had broken into the room of a country inn where the young schoolgirl lay asleep. 'I had a small but sharp knife with me. I held the child's head and cut her throat. I heard the blood spurt. It spurted in an arch, right over my head,' Kurten told police interrogators. And as he matter-of-factly described his first heinous crime, detectives noted that his eyes gazed longingly and wistfully at the pale throat of the young female stenographer who was making a record of his gruesome confessions!

No doubt Kurten's thoughts were flashing back to the early morning hours of a summer's day in 1913 when ten-year-old Christine Klein was murdered as she lay sleeping in her bedroom above the tavern run by her father in the picturesque town of Koln-Mulheim, one of the most beautiful spots in the Rhine River valley.

The immediate suspect in the killing of little Christine was her Uncle Otto. The evening before the vicious slaying Otto had an argument with Christine's father

Peter. Otto had asked his brother Peter for a loan, but had been turned down. There was a bitter quarrel, at the height of which Otto threatened to do something that his brother 'would remember all of his life'.

Naturally these words came back to haunt Otto with a vengeance after his young niece was found brutally slain in her bed. Left in the room was one major clue – a handkerchief embroidered with the initials PK. Since the girl's father, Peter Klein, was far from being a suspect, detectives surmised that Otto might have borrowed the handkerchief from his brother. Police were convinced hot-tempered Otto had something to do with the murder since there was no other apparent motive and the innocent young victim didn't have an enemy in the world.

A coroner's report revealed that the girl had been sexually molested, but there was no evidence of actual rape. She had been choked into unconsciousness, her throat slit, and her private parts invaded by rough fingers, according to the medical examiner's findings. Police theorized that Otto might have violated the girl's genitals to make it look as if she was the victim of a sexually motivated assault.

The strongest part of the prosecution's case against Otto, however, were the wild and violent threats he had made in front of several witnesses only hours before the slaying. They felt that circumstantial evidence, along with opportunity, was enough to charge him with Christine's murder.

A judge and jury didn't think the case against Otto was strong enough, however, and he was acquitted when it came to trial. It would be almost three decades before Christine Klein's killer was eventually brought to justice – bringing with it the end of the reign of terror of the infamous Vampire of Düsseldorf.

The Düsseldorf slayings began sixteen years after the killing of Christine Klein. The city's first sex crime was an attack on a woman called Kuhn. She didn't get a chance to identify her mystery assailant, who grabbed her by the lapels and pushed her to the ground in a dimly lit street. As she screamed and struggled, the dark figure lurking over her stabbed her quickly several times before running away. Young Frau Kuhn lived to have nightmares about her experience, although she was hospitalized for three months until twenty-four gaping stab wounds healed.

Not so lucky was eight-year-old Rosa Ohliger, whose mutilated body was found partially concealed under a hedge on the outskirts of the city. Her savaged body shocked even the most hardened detectives on the crime scene. Not only had the little girl been sexually assaulted, as the semen stains on her undergarments demonstrated, she had also been stabbed repeatedly in the vagina with a sharp weapon, later identified as a pair of scissors. Altogether, she had been stabbed thirteen times. Then her naked body had been doused with petrol and a clumsy attempt made to burn the corpse.

Not even the men of the city were safe. A week after the Ohliger killing a forty-five-year-old mechanic called Scheer was found stabbed to death by the roadside in the suburb of Flingern. He had bled to death from twenty stab wounds, many of them to his head.

Police were sure their problems were over and their citizenry safe at last when a half-witted man called Stausberg attacked two women and was arrested shortly afterwards. Stausberg obligingly also confessed to the murders of Ohliger and Scheer and was locked away in a mental home.

Investigators realized the half-wit Stausberg couldn't have been the perpetrator when, six months later, the monstrous killer struck again – this time attacking a group of people, a man of thirty, a girl of eighteen, a woman of thirty, as they were walking home together one evening. All three were stabbed but, fortunately, none of them sustained serious injury.

On 24 August 1929, the monster struck again in earnest. Two young girls, five-year-old Gertrude Hamacher and fourteen-year-old Louise Lenzen, who had been to a fair in the city suburb of Flehe, were stalked by a dark shadow as they walked hand in hand back home in the early evening. They were later found lying like abandoned rag dolls, just a few feet from the footpath through a neighbourhood community vegetable garden. Both had been throttled, then their throats cut.

The following day, only a few miles away, a third girl was accosted and was lucky to escape with her life. Twenty-six-year-old Gertrude Schulte, a servant girl, described how she was approached by a pleasant-looking but plain man of about forty who asked if she would like to go with him to a fair in the town of Neuss.

Foolishly she accepted his invitation, but on the way there he dragged her into the woods and demanded that she have sexual intercourse with him. When Fräulein Schulte boldly retorted, 'I'd rather die', her assailant cried out, 'Die then!' and proceeded to stab her about the head and body with such force that his knife broke, leaving part of the blade embedded in her neck. She managed to remain conscious, screaming her head off all the while, until her attacker fled. A passer-by heard her screaming and she was taken to hospital where she recovered.

The Düsseldorf demon stepped up his attacks late into summer. Women were scared to go out – even in broad daylight – without an escort. At night no women or children were seen on the streets. Doors were heavily bolted, and curtains were drawn. The daring and dastardly escapades of the Vampire of Düsseldorf began making international headlines.

For Düsseldorf 1929 was a year of terror. By then, the faceless, nameless vampire that stalked at night had committed almost fifty acts of perversion, each one during a vicious attack. At least five people ended up being taken to mortuaries. Medical experts were convinced the vampire had lost all control over his sadistic tendencies.

In September, another young servant girl, Ida Reuter, was raped and bludgeoned to death with a hammer. The following month, yet another servant lass, Elisabeth Dorrier, was also battered to death.

A young woman out for a walk was asked by a stranger if she was not afraid to be walking alone – then was knocked unconscious with a hammer before she could reply. That same evening, a prostitute was also beaten unconscious by a maniac wielding a hammer.

The city's feared predator became more brazen and bolder with each attack, as if he was draining energy from his victims and growing stronger and stronger.

He started to crave publicity, and in effect became his own publicity agent. When five-year-old Gertrude Albermann disappeared, the Düsseldorf communist newspaper *Freedom* received a letter saying that the child's body was dumped amidst bricks and rubble near a local factory. The informant enclosed a map. He also gave directions to a local field called Pappendelle meadows where he said another missing girl was to be found.

Unfortunately, the fiendish informant was right on both counts. Toddler Gertrude Albermann's body was buried under rubble next to a factory wall just as he had described; she had been slashed thirty-six times and fiendishly mutilated. In the Pappendelle meadows, a search party uncovered the nude body of servant girl, Maria Hahn, who had been missing for months; she too had been viciously stabbed and hacked to death.

There's no telling how long Kurten could have continued his stalking and slaying if he had not been caught, almost by sheer chance.

A letter was delivered to a Frau Brugmann in Düsseldorf on 19 May 1930. It was from a twenty-year-old domestic servant girl called Maria Budlick and should have been delivered to a Frau Bruckner, but the name was misspelled and the strange letter arrived at Frau Brugmann's address instead.

The letter told a bizarre story. In it, young Maria described a truly weird adventure she had had only two days previously. Maria said she had travelled from Cologne to Düsseldorf seeking employment. On the train she had met Frau Bruckner, who had promised to help her find a job. That was why Maria Budlick was writing to her.

She related the following intervening episode. After she got separated from Frau Bruckner in Düsseldorf railway station, the innocent newcomer to the city was accosted by a man who offered to help her find a bed for the night. Alone and lonely in new surroundings, she agreed and the man led the young servant girl across the city, through the busy streets and into the darkness of the city's Volksgarten Park. Only then did the stories about the notorious Düsseldorf vampire start flooding into her mind and she turned cold. Sensing she was in jeopardy, she was just about to scream for help when a kind-looking stranger came to her rescue. The stranger questioned her escort's intentions, and the man slunk off into the night. Maria Budlick was left in the park with a new stranger in her life. It turned out her switch took her out of the frying-pan and put her into the fire.

First of all, the so-called kind stranger wanted to take her back to his room in a house in nearby Mettmanner Strasse. Naïve and frightened, Maria walked with him to that address, but once she got to his home she sensed that his intentions were also dishonourable. After he gave her a ham sandwich and a glass of milk, Maria refused his invitation to stay with him overnight in his room. She demanded the man take her to a hostel for young women.

He agreed, but on the way there he took her to a

deserted park – the city's Grafenburg woods this time – where he embraced her roughly, forced a kiss on her, then asked pointblank for sex. Her attacker told her bluntly, 'Do you know where you are? I can tell you! You are alone with me in the middle of the woods. Now you can scream as much as you like and no one will hear you.'

Terrified, Maria agreed to have sex with him, and he pulled down her undergarments. They had sex standing up. Afterwards, he asked her casually, 'In case there's anything you might need and I can help, do you remember my address?'

Maria's wisest move that evening was answering 'No' – a reply that undoubtedly saved her life. Her attacker then surprisingly led her back to a brightly lit thoroughfare and abandoned her beside a street-car stop. She was able to make her way to a hostel run by nuns where she was given refuge for the night.

Frau Brugmann, who accidentally intercepted and read this bizarre letter to Frau Bruckner, was shocked and upset by its contents. To her the incident smacked of rape, rather than an amorous interlude. She took the letter straight to Chief Inspector Gennat, the detective in charge of investigations into the Vampire of Düsseldorf slayings.

Maria Budlick's letter intrigued Inspector Gennat. It was a slender lead, but a lead none the less. He sought out young Maria Budlick and asked her to take him to the home of the stranger who lived in Mettmanner Strasse.

With difficulty, Maria eventually led the policeman to the hallway of a building at No. 71 Mettmanner Strasse, and haltingly suggested that she thought this might be the right place. Only when the landlord allowed Budlick and Inspector Gennat into one of the rooms did she recognize it as the place to which the stranger in the park had brought her only a few nights before.

Heading out of the building, Maria and the Inspector almost bumped into the amorous stranger on the stairway. He blanched when he saw her and her police escort, then quickly turned on his heels and scurried out of the building.

But he was a marked man. The landlady was able to give the police his name: Peter Kurten. She was only able to supply sketchy details about her tenant Kurten's background. Neighbours knew him to be pleasant, a likeable sort, who was particularly popular with children. On the down side, he had a reputation as a womanizer. He lived with his wife in an apartment on the top floor of the building and was known to be frequently unfaithful to her.

Since Kurten had effectively vanished into thin air, police turned their attention to his wife. They fetched Frau Kurten from the restaurant where she worked late most nights. But there was little the big-boned, middle-aged hausfrau could tell them – other than the fact her husband had been in trouble with the law before, for a variety of offences ranging from burglary to sexual indecency.

However, the police hadn't heard the last of Frau Kurten. A few days later, on 24 May 1930, she showed up at the police station with a dramatic nugget of information: her husband, Peter Kurten, was the homicidal Vampire of Düsseldorf.

He had confessed this to her, said Frau Kurten, when he returned home after fleeing the Maria Budlick confrontation. She had refused to believe him at first, thinking he was joking. He had eventually convinced her he was the killer all Europe was looking for. At first she had broken down and cried, Frau Kurten told the police. She loved her husband, and did not relish the thought of him being taken away, leaving her alone and penniless. She had suggested a suicide pact, but Kurten had dismissed that idea, telling her instead that she could become a rich woman by turning him in and claiming the reward.

After much argument, he persuaded her that was the best plan of action. Police accompanied Frau Kurten to a predetermined meeting place outside Düsseldorf's St Rochus Church at three o'clock that afternoon. Kurten was standing nonchalantly on the sidewalk, and merely smiled wryly as four policemen converged on him brandishing revolvers. 'Don't worry – I'm not planning to go anywhere,' Kurten told them as they pushed him around, slamming handcuffs on his wrists. Only then did the full mystery and horror story of this elusive enigma called Peter Kurten begin unravelling.

Kurten established a close bond with police psychiatrist Professor Karl Berg, and poured out his heart to the good doctor, who was spellbound by the atrocities described to him by the affable Kurten.

Kurten began by telling the Professor about his awful childhood. Born in Koln-Mulheim, the son of the town drunk, and brought up as one of thirteen children in a run-down one-room apartment, he was exposed to the sexual act at an early age. His alcoholic father frequently had sexual relations with his wife in full view of the children. Eventually his father was jailed for three years after attempting to rape his thirteen-year-old daughter. Whereupon his mother obtained a divorce and remarried.

Kurten confessed that watching his father's drunken sexual bouts excited him even as a small child. He suspected that, like his father, he too was oversexed. The best friend he remembered as a child was a degenerate older youth, the local dog-catcher, who had taught him to torture and masturbate the dogs, and explained the mysteries and joys of sex to him when he was only eight years old. Even at that age, inflamed with sexual excitement, he tried to have intercourse with his sister – the same girl his drunken father had assaulted.

He also displayed a homicidal rage at an early age. When he was five, he pushed a playmate off a raft into the river Rhine. Another playmate jumped in to rescue the drowning boy. Kurten fought them off as they tried to get back on board the raft. He even held their heads under the water in an attempt to drown them. Who would ever have suspected that the innocent-faced five-year-old could be a callous killer.

By the age of thirteen, he was heavily into sexual deviation, practising bestiality with sheep, pigs and goats. This led to more gory perversions, particularly those associated with blood. He found that he got the most powerful sexual sensation when he stabbed a sheep to death as he was having intercourse with the animal.

This act he performed repeatedly in his early teens.

He ran away from home at the age of sixteen after stealing money from his mother. He had little recourse but to embark on a life of crime. He wasn't a very successful criminal, and it was only months after he ran away from home that he received the first of seventeen prison sentences that were to take up twenty-four years of his life.

Rebellious and insubordinate as a young prisoner, Kurten was sentenced to long periods of solitary confinement. He survived these spells of loneliness by daydreaming, acting out the most horrifying sexual fantasies in his warped teenage mind.

He ached for the opportunity to vent the sadistic urges he felt towards farm animals on human beings. His depraved sexual education was completed when he latched on to a veteran prostitute, twice his age, who happened to be a masochist and was receptive to Kurten's perverted acts of brutality. They made a fine team. Kurten eventually moved in with her and, for a while, his perverse sexual urges were being attended to in private.

But it was only a matter of time before young Kurten would crave fresh blood, leading him to kill again. And this time it was a blood-thirsty, predatory killing . . . choking and slitting the throat of ten-year-old Christine Klein as she slept in bed in her bedroom above the tavern in Kurten's own home town. As he sliced the little girl's throat and blood began spurting, he experienced a sexual orgasm. He left behind a vital clue which could have put an early end to his diabolical career. But the clue was misread – it was the handkerchief bearing the initials PK.

So Peter Kurten was left free to continue his blood-thirsty course through life, free to roam the area in and around Düsseldorf for the next eighteen years . . . hacking, bludgeoning, strangling, raping and mutilating scores of unsuspecting victims. Female victims, like Maria Budlick, who were fortunate enough to survive his sadistic attacks recalled him whispering to them as he squeezed their windpipes, 'That's what love's about.' Kurten explained that just the thrill of strangling a woman brought him to orgasm.

Kurten was more than candid with his inquisitor, Professor Berg, who also made copious notes as Kurten related his life story. These notes were later to be used as the research for a classic book Professor Berg was to write on psychopathic killers.

Thousands of sightseers lined up for a seat in the vast converted drill hall adjacent to Düsseldorf police head-quarters where the trial of this dapper, but nondescript man who had held an entire city in the grip of fear was to take place. The fortunate ones, who made it into the trial – which began in a great fanfare of publicity on 13 April 1931 – saw Kurten, who stood accused of nine murders, seven attempted murders, and a whole battery of assaults, give more than a hint of self-pride as he freely confessed to his monstrous life devoted to depravity and perversion. They shuddered as they heard him reveal that the taking of blood was the motivating force behind his crimes. Blood sexually excited him. On several occasions he drank his victims' blood, he said – on one occasion enough to make him violently ill. He admitted drinking blood directly from the throat of one victim; from a wound on the temple of another. During another attack, he remembered greedily licking the blood from his injured victim's hands.

At one point, the judge interrupted this seemingly endless monologue of confession to ask him why he had committed these awful crimes. With a theatrical flourish, Kurten swept his hand to his heart, pointed, and exclaimed, 'Gentlemen, to find out, you must look in here!'

A stunned and shaken courtroom blenched as Kurten – enclosed in a specially constructed, escape-proof cage – calmly went on to tell how he once reached a sexual climax by decapitating a swan in a public park, then put his greedy mouth over the headless neck to gulp down the torrent of blood.

As he continued talking in his almost gentle, modulated voice, court officials' and spectators' blood ran ice-cold as they realized that Kurten's crimes and perversions were even more monstrous than they first suspected. He wasn't just a mere psychopath. He was a walking textbook of depravity – a sex maniac, a vampire, an arsonist, a strangler, a rapist, a hammer-wielding sadist, a knife-slashing fiend, a man who confessed to enjoyment from bestiality, a man who achieved orgasms merely witnessing gory street accidents, and got sexual satisfaction out of fantasizing about disasters which claimed the lives of thousands.

Spectators thought they were listening to a lecture by Satan himself, as Kurten, in a calm monotone, related some of his unrealized desires: 'I thought of myself causing accidents affecting thousands of people. And I invented a number of crazy fantasies such as smashing bridges and boring through bridge piers. I imagined myself using schools and orphanages where I could carry out murders by giving away chocolate samples containing arsenic.'

Defence psychiatrists claimed Kurten had to be insane. But a numbed jury, after only an hour's deliberation, had no hesitation in sentencing the Monster of Düsseldorf – as he enjoyed calling himself – to be guillotined. He was sentenced to death nine times, in fact.

With characteristic, ghoulish curiosity, blood-obsessed Kurten looked up from the enormous last meal he was devouring with relish to ask the prison psychiatrist shortly before his execution: 'After my head has been chopped off, will I be able to hear – at least for a moment – the sound of my blood gushing through the stump of my neck?'

Without waiting for an answer, he savoured that horrific thought for a moment, then observed quietly: 'That would be the pleasure to end all pleasures.'

Kurten made his walk to the guillotine on 2 July 1931.

BELA KISS

Did vampire killer of twenty-seven women return from the dead?

Budapest, Hungary   What better name for a real-life vampire than Bela Kiss – and a Hungarian as well?!

Hungarians brought up on tales of wild-eyed vampires which haunt the wild Carpathian mountain region of their native land are easily persuaded that forty-two-year-old Bela Kiss, who vanished shortly after the outbreak of the First World War, was indeed one of the living-dead. A prosperous tinsmith from the village of Czinkota, a few miles from Budapest, Kiss was never brought to justice for his bizarre and horrifying crimes. And many villagers believe he still walks among us, an ageless, predatory demon!

Kiss turned from a pillar of the community into a bitter recluse after his beautiful, blonde wife Maria mysteriously vanished without a trace. Not long after that villager Isabelle Koblitz, niece of the nation's Minister of Commerce disappeared from her home. And a young woman called Luisa Ruszt reported being

attacked by a wild-eyed monster, fangs bared and bab-
bling incoherently, who jumped out at her as she walked
along a moonlit street. She managed to escape his
clutches and ran for her life.

Soon after the outbreak of war, the eccentric villager
Bela Kiss surprised his neighbours when he enlisted in
the Hungarian army. Six months after he had signed up,
villagers received a notification that he had been killed in
action.

While disposing of his property, neighbours uncovered the dark, secret life of Kiss. A search of his
rambling old house revealed a number of fuel drums.
Opening one containing industrial alcohol, they were
appalled to see staring up at them the preserved and
beautiful face of his long-lost wife.

Four other drums also held bodies. Police from
Budapest came to the scene and ordered the area
around Kiss' house of secrets excavated. A total of
twenty-six more bodies of young women were
unearthed. Like in Maria's case, the cause of death in
each instance was strangulation, but what intrigued
investigators more were the series of sharp wounds on
the necks of each victim – all of whom had been
drained of their blood.

Other, more fortunate women began to come forward
to identify Kiss as their evil vampire attacker.

Then the plot took a dramatic and mysterious twist
when detectives went to the wartime hospital where the
fugitive vampire was supposed to have died from war
wounds. The head nurse there listened open-mouthed as
police described their suspect. 'But the patient who died

was only twenty. It could not have been Bela Kiss!' she gasped.

Did the evil Kiss switch identities with the dead young soldier to escape justice? Police files on Bela Kiss have never been closed.

NEVILLE HEATH

An officer and a gentleman
. . . with a bloodlust

Handsome Neville George Clevely Heath, who loved to pose as a suave, heroic air force officer, had no trouble attracting the ladies. If only his pretty victims had known that his easy charm and worldly good looks masked a monster with a lust for blood. This twenty-nine-year-old sadistic fantasist, with an insatiable, almost reckless lust for blood, was soon christened 'The Gentleman Vampire' by the imaginative crime reporters of the British tabloid press.

On the evening of 20 June 1946, using the names Lieutenant Colonel and Mrs G.C. Heath, he booked into room number four in the Pembridge Court Hotel, an inexpensive but popular rendezvous hotel in Notting Hill Gate in London. His companion was Margery Aimee Brownell Gardner, an amateur artist and would-be movie star, who had a penchant for flagellation, bondage and other masochistic activities.

Gardner was a married woman, but separated from

her husband. She enjoyed the bohemian life of post-war London's laugh, drink and be merry nightclub society. In fact, on the eve of her death, she had dined, drunk and danced the night away with gay blade Heath at the Panama Club in fashionable South Kensington.

A cab driver who picked them up at the club and took them to the hotel came forward later. An excellent eyewitness, cabbie Harry Harter not only remembered his fare and his tip down to the last penny – but was able to place Heath and Gardner arm-in-arm entering the Pembridge Court Hotel, laughing and joking together.

The fact that the unfortunate, thirty-three-year-old Margery, whose only film exposure to date had been as an extra in a few obscure B-movies, had a predilection for kinky sex played right into the hands of the vampirish nature of blood-thirsty sadist Heath.

The next day 'Colonel Heath' had vanished . . . leaving behind the brutalized body of Miss Gardner.

First on the gruesome scene was Alice Wyatt, who helped her father run the nineteen-bedroom hotel. Called upstairs by an anxious maid, Mrs Wyatt saw Margery Gardner's dark hair protruding from beneath casually tossed bedclothes in one of the room's two single beds. Pulling the sheets up, Mrs Wyatt reeled when she saw the young woman's scarred and bloody naked torso.

She had been suffocated and the gag was still jammed in her mouth. Her flesh was covered with blood oozing from strange, diamond-patterned whip marks. Curiously, her face had been washed or licked clean of blood, although congealed blood still clogged her nostrils.

There was no evidence that sexual intercourse had taken place, but her nipples had been bitten off, and her vagina torn and mutilated by the insertion of some kind of blunt instrument which apparently had been fiercely rotated. Her ankles were bound tightly together with a handkerchief.

The other single bed in the room was even more sodden with blood, suggesting that the more serious injuries had been caused there, and the body lifted over to the other bed afterwards.

Famed London forensic scientist Dr Keith Simpson was immediately called to the blood-spattered hotel room. Professor Simpson summed up the sado-masochistic nature of the crime immediately, but was particularly interested in the seventeen cruelly and deliberately administered, distinctive whip marks – obviously caused by some kind of patterned thong with a metal tip – which criss-crossed Margery Gardner's naked and mutilated body.

'Find that whip and you've got your man,' Dr Simpson quietly told detectives after performing an autopsy on the corpse at the nearby Hammersmith Hospital. Despite the awful blood-drawing injuries which had all been inflicted before her death, Dr Simpson concluded that the real cause of death was suffocation – either by the gag, a pillow, or the bedclothes, or by having her head pressed, face-down, into the pillow.

The graphic horror of the discovery had post-war London in a panic. Scotland Yard knew it had a depraved monster on the loose. It also didn't take them long to link the name on the hotel register to Heath, already known to the police as a man with a record – although never for anything violent. Thanks to cab driver Harter, other witnesses from the Panama Club, the Pembridge Court Hotel, and the hotel register, Scotland Yard detectives were pretty confident that Heath was their man, and an all-points bulletin was issued for his arrest.

Police visited Heath's parents' home in the London suburb of Wimbledon and took possession of a selection of photographs of Heath in a number of uniforms. But they decided against publishing them in the newspapers in case their pre-trial publication jeopardized the possibility of an eventual murder conviction. Unfortunately, that legally influenced decision was to delay Heath's capture and cost another young woman her life.

Obviously excited by his blood-thirsty initiation to murder at the London hotel, it did not take Heath long to strike again. On the run under an assumed name, he struck in the seaside town of Bournemouth, less than 100 miles from the capital. He checked into the Tollard Royal Hotel on Sunday, 23 June 1946, this time as 'Group Captain Rupert Brooke' – ironically the name of the sensitive and heroic First World War soldier-poet.

For thirteen carefree days – until Saturday, 6 July – the good-looking six-footer became a popular and well-known face at the Tollard Royal Hotel. To the staff, he was obviously a free-spending officer and gentleman. To other men he was a war hero, a true man's man; and there were few women who failed to comment on his twinkling blue eyes, fair wavy hair, and dimpled features. He also ran up a generous hotel tab and restaurant and bar bill that was to remain unpaid.

He struck up a special rapport with a new lady friend, twenty-one-year-old Doreen Marshall, a lonely guest at the neighbouring Norfolk Hotel. Her wealthy father had sent Doreen – a pretty, petite but frail young lass – there to recover from a bout of influenza. Heath first met her while out on a morning stroll. Glib-tongued and impeccably dressed 'Group Captain Brooke' had no trouble striking up a conversation with the impressionable Miss Marshall, and talked the pretty former Womens' Royal Navy recruit into being his guest for lunch; then dinner later that evening. Nor did he have any trouble convincing her to allow him to accompany her on a harmless after-dinner stroll in the early morning hours of Thursday, 4 July, ostensibly to escort her safely back to her hotel. That was the last time Doreen Marshall was seen alive.

Ivan Relf, the manager of the Tollard Royal Hotel remembered a young woman leaving with the 'Group Captain' after dinner. He seemed to remember the 'Group Captain' appearing to be a little tipsy, but the woman did not seem to be in good humour. The night porter recalled Heath telling him he was walking the lady home and would be back in half an hour, but the slightly built young lady – who had said she would have preferred to have gone home herself by taxi – snapped, 'Quarter of an hour.'

In truth, no one could recall when the 'Group Captain' returned to the hotel. (It was later established that Heath had arrived back at the hotel in the early morning hours and gained access to his room unseen by climbing a ladder and clambering through a window.)

It was a couple of days, getting close to the week-end, before the manager of the Norfolk Hotel, where Miss Marshall had been staying, called his friend, manager Relf of the Tollard Royal, to tell him one of his guests was missing – and that he had been told she had had dinner at the Tollard Royal on Wednesday evening.

Relf recalled his 'Group Captain' having dinner with a young lady, but, when quizzed, Heath told the manager that his guest had certainly not been Miss Marshall, but a woman he had known for some time. Since he had no other reason to doubt this, manager Relf let the matter drop.

All hell suddenly broke loose five days after Miss Marshall's disappearance when the swarming of flies around a patch of undergrowth on a quiet path near the hotel aroused the suspicions of passers-by. On investigation, Miss Marshall's body was found dumped in a clump of rhododendron bushes, naked except for a yellow left shoe. Her clothing was casually draped over her body as if it had been tossed nonchalantly on top of her. Her empty handbag found nearby had been rifled for items of value.

The pathetic corpse was covered in blood and had been mutilated with a knife. In some cases, the stab wounds were an inch deep, and her throat was slit in two places causing severe haemorrhaging – the probable cause of death. Her body had obviously been pinioned to the ground by the body weight of a much stronger person during the attack – Miss Marshall was only 5 ft. 3 ins. –

and her hands were slashed where she had tried to fend off her crazed, more powerful, assailant. Her nipples were partially bitten off, and a jagged series of slashes reached from her vagina vertically up to her chest. Another jagged weapon, probably a branch from a nearby bush, had been used to violate and perforate both her vagina and her anus.

The tree or bush branch and knife were never found, giving rise to speculation that the killer had disposed of these weapons in the sea. From descriptions given by staff at the London and Bournemouth hotels, the police needed little convincing that their suspect Heath had struck again, and since no blood was ever found on Heath's clothing, detectives were convinced he stripped himself naked before the attack, then washed his blood-spattered body in the sea after committing the dastardly deed.

Incredibly, detectives did not have to look far for their suspect. Heath literally gave himself up. He called Bournemouth police station, identified himself as Brooke, and said if they had a photograph of Doreen Marshall he might be able to help them with their inquiries.

Delighted at getting such an amazing early break in the case, the detectives invited him down to the police station where he was promptly detained for questioning about the Gardner murder. It didn't take the investigators long to recognize 'Group Captain Brooke' as the fugitive Heath from the London murder of a few weeks ago.

However, playing along with him, they questioned

him first about the unfortunate Miss Marshall. Heath/ Brooke eventually admitted knowing the young woman and acknowledged he had taken her for dinner the night before her disappearance. After they left the Tollard Royal Hotel together, said Heath, they sat for a short time on a bench overlooking the sea. He left her near Bournemouth Pier and watched her head off in the direction of the Norfolk Hotel. He then returned to his hotel – and used a ladder to get into his room by way of playing a trick on the night porter.

Needless to say, the attentive detectives did not buy this cock and bull story for one minute. And since he was still insisting his name was Brooke, Detective Inspector George Gates eventually sighed and told him: 'I am satisfied you are Neville George Clevely Heath, and I am going to detain you pending the arrival of the London Metropolitan Police.'

'Oh, all right,' retorted Heath with a bored air of finality.

When Detective Inspector Reg Spooner arrived from London, Heath adopted an air of complete indifference. Asked about the murder of Margery Gardner, he said first of all: 'I might make a statement after I've had some sleep.' Then when told he was going to be taken to London, he decided: 'I really have nothing to say at the moment.'

Heath was searched and a left-luggage ticket for property left at Bournemouth railway station was found in his pocket. It led police to an attaché case containing a riding whip with a distinctive plaited thong – one of the weapons used in the brutalization and slaying of Margery

Gardner. Also in the case was a scarf caked in blood – Margery Gardner's blood.

Further investigation soon linked him to Doreen Marshall's disappearance and murder. A handkerchief sodden with Miss Marshall's blood was found in a drawer in his hotel room. And a local pawnbroker reported Heath had pawned a ring belonging to Miss Marshall in the past thirty-six hours. Another damning clue found in Heath's possession was the return half of a first-class ticket to London which had been the property of Doreen Marshall. Heath lamely claimed he had found the ticket on a seat in the lounge of the Tollard Royal Hotel.

He was further incriminated by Tollard Hotel employees. The night porter remembered seeing Heath's shoes caked with mud outside his room in the early hours of the morning Miss Marshall vanished, and other staff members recalled how the following day 'Group Captain Brooke' took to wearing a silk scarf. Obviously to conceal a number of fresh scratches on his neck.

As the Scotland Yard murder squad detective in charge of the Notting Hill investigation, Superintendent Thomas Barratt, had collected quite a dossier on Heath since the first murder, the investigators were anxious to find more about the missing month between the London hotel murder and the date Heath checked in as Brooke at the Bournemouth hotel. They had by now established that Heath was an inveterate womanizer with a violent, sadistic attitude towards women.

It transpired that Heath had been involved in a violent episode with Margery Gardner on another evening, a few weeks before he killed her, and that she had been rescued by an alert house detective. Whatever possessed her to return to the Pembridge Court Hotel with a sadist like Heath, no one will ever know.

On the police blotter was also a report of another unrelated sadistic incident involving the suspect Heath. A few weeks before the Gardner murder, police were called to a hotel in London's Strand where a woman reported that Heath had bound and flogged her. But embarrassed about the possible publicity, she had declined to press charges against the fiend-in-waiting. Thus, the police had good reason to fear Heath might have claimed other less-fortunate victims during that missing month.

Heath had been with yet another woman friend during that period but, amazingly, had not harmed her or given her any kind of clue he was on the run from a brutal sex crime.

Apparently, after the Notting Hill murder, he had fled to the quiet south coast seaside town of Worthing where he booked into the Ocean Hotel. He looked up a local resident, nineteen-year-old Yvonne Symonds, another of his recent conquests, whom he had also wined and dined at the Panama Club and shared a night of passion with – surprisingly, no kinky sex was involved – at the now notorious Pembridge Court Hotel.

Unsuspecting Yvonne had obviously not seen the London newspapers when she lunched with Heath in Worthing. During the meal he told her that there had been 'a nasty murder' at their love-nest hotel. And because he knew the victim, said Heath, he had been helping the police in the investigation.

Albert Fish, the deranged
killer of Grace Budd

Assistant District Attorney
Francis Morrow, Fish and
Detective William King, the
man who was obsessed with
solving Grace Budd's
murder

Neville George Clevely Heath, dashing RAF pilot and vicious killer

Doreen Marshall, who was persuaded by Neville Heath to allow him to accompany her back to her hotel. She was never seen alive again

Police photograph the body of Doreen Marshall

James Riva, self-proclaimed vampire, stands in court as the jury pronounces him guilty of the murder of his grandmother

John G. Haigh on his way to court

Dr Archibald Henderson and his wife Rose, victims of John Haigh

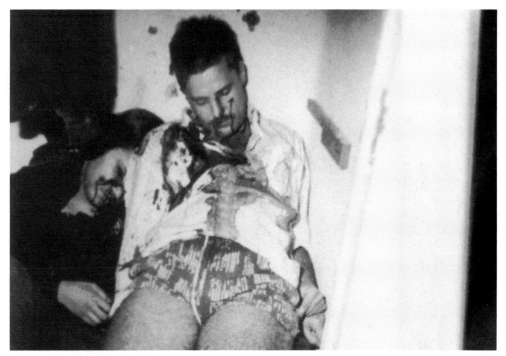

Adolfo de Jesus Constanzo and his homosexual lover, Martin Quintana
Rodriguez, shot dead after a violent siege and shoot-out with the police

Fritz Haarmann, the 'Vampire of Hanover', handcuffed between two
policemen as an International Newsreel cameraman films

The lovely Elizabeth Short who would soon become more famous in death as the 'Black Dahlia'

Elizabeth Short and Major Matt Gordon. This photograph was found in her trunk after her death

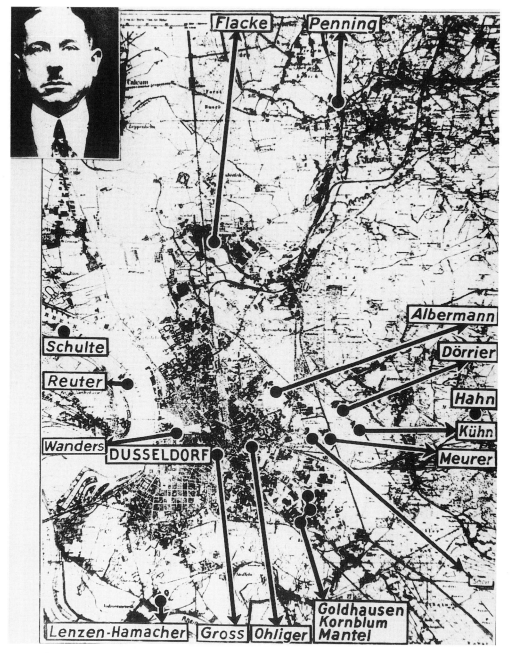

This police map of Düsseldorf plots the murders committed by Peter Kurten (*top left*)

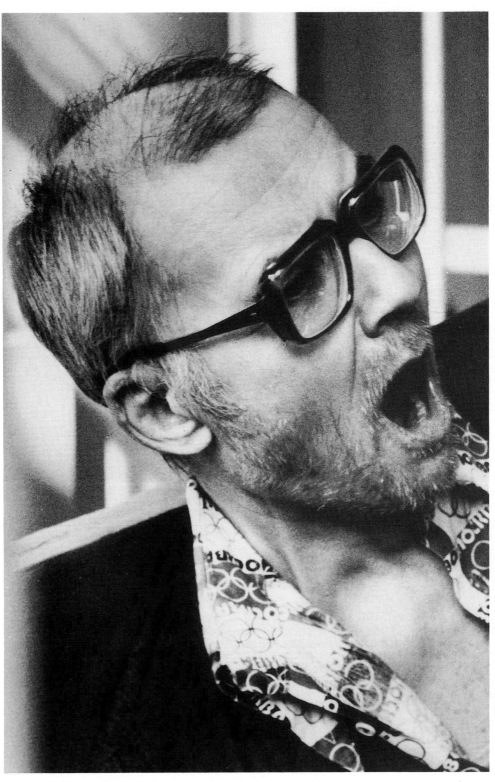

Andrei Chikatilo, the 'Rostov Ripper', yawns loudly as the judge reads out the guilty verdict. Chikatilo was found guilty of 53 sex murders

'How did the girl die?' Miss Symonds asked Heath, never for one second doubting her debonair and charming lover.

'A poker was stuck up her,' replied Heath bluntly. 'I think that's what killed her – although Superintendent Barratt seems to believe she might have been suffocated.'

Horrified, his luncheon companion held her hand to her mouth and gasped, 'What sort of person would commit an awful crime like that?'

Heath replied, shrugging: 'A sex maniac, I suppose.'

After lunch, Heath, who by this time had proposed marriage to Miss Symonds, took her home safely, gentlemanly depositing her at her parents' doorstep with a chaste kiss.

Even after she read in the London newspapers about the Notting Hill slaying, Miss Symonds still did not dream for one moment that her beloved Neville had anything to do with it. She called him at his hotel to tell him, 'My parents are very worried about what they're reading in the papers.'

Playing his man-of-the-world role to the hilt, he reassured her, 'I thought they might be . . . but I've got myself a car and I'm driving back up to London to try and sort this whole mess out. I'll give you a ring from there.'

Heath did not ring his alarmed fiancée from London, though. He didn't even go to London. Instead he caught a train to Bournemouth further up the coast – and a deadly appointment with the unsuspecting Doreen Marshall.

Before leaving Worthing, in a last-ditch effort to cover his tracks, the cunning Heath sent a red-herring letter to Superintendent Barratt at Scotland Yard. It read:

Sir,

I feel it is my duty to inform you of certain facts in connection with the death of Mrs Gardner at Notting Hill Gate. I booked in at that hotel last Sunday, but not with Mrs Gardner whom I met for the first time during the week. I had drinks with her on Friday evening, and whilst I was with her she met an acquaintance with whom she was obliged to sleep. The reasons, as I understand them, were mainly financial.

It was then that Mrs Gardner asked if she could use my hotel room until two o'clock that morning and intimated that, if I returned after that, I might spend the remainder of the night with her. I gave her my key and told her to keep the hotel room door unlocked. It must have been almost 3 a.m. when I returned to the hotel and found her in the condition of which you are aware. I realized I was in an invidious position, and rather than notify the police I packed my belongings and left.

Since then I've been in several minds whether to come forward or not. But in view of the circumstances, I've been afraid to. I can give you a description of the man. He was aged approximately thirty, dark hair (black), with a small moustache. Height about 5 ft. 9 ins., slim build. His name was

Jack, and I gathered he was a friend of Mrs Gardner's of some long standing.

The personal column of the *Daily Telegraph* will find me, but at the moment I have assumed another name. I should like to come forward and help, but I cannot face the music of a trumped-up charge which will obviously be preferred against me if I should do so. I have the instrument with which Mrs Gardner was beaten and am forwarding this to you today. You will find my fingerprints on it, but you should find others as well.

N.G.C. Heath

The parcel containing the weapon of death never arrived. And Heath proceeded to his next destination – as the vacationing Group Captain Brooke at Bournemouth.

Heath's background, by this time very well-known to the police, was a colourful one. He was born in Ilford, Essex, in 1917. His father was a barber and his mother the dominant force in the Heath household. He was educated at a local Catholic school where he had a reputation as a bully and a tormentor of animals. He excelled at sports, but never applied himself to his academic studies and left school for a series of minor jobs. He was compulsively sticky-fingered, and continually in trouble with the police for dishonesty, although never for violent crimes.

That dishonest streak stayed with him later when he tried to improve his station in life and became a young army and air force officer, in his native England and in

South Africa. Both times he was court-martialled and discharged for dishonourable conduct.

Here is an excerpt from his ten-year chequered career of military service and crime as outlined in his Scotland Yard dossier:

February 1936   Obtained short-service commission in the Royal Air Force.

August 1937   Court-martialled for being absent without leave for nearly five months. Other charges included escaping while under arrest and 'borrowing' a non-commissioned officer's car without permission. Sentence to be cashiered. Commuted subsequently to dismissal.

November 1937   Placed on probation for fraudulently obtaining credit at a Nottingham hotel and attempting to obtain a car by false pretences. Eight other offences, including posing as a certain 'Lord Dudley', were taken into account.

July 1938   Sentenced to three years Borstal training for housebreaking and stealing jewellery from a friend and for obtaining clothing using a forged banker's order. Ten other offences taken into account.

September 1939   Released because of the outbreak of war. (Years later, while in the service, he was to return to the Borstal as an army officer and give the young inmates a lecture on how it was possible to turn your life around and make good.)

October 1939   Enlisted in Royal Army Service Corps.

March 1940   Commissioned, and posted to the Middle East.

July 1941   Placed under arrest after a dispute with a brigadier. Went absent without leave. Court-martialled for these offences and for obtaining a second pay-book by false pretences; making a false statement to his commanding officer, thus enabling him to be absent from his unit; and five other charges related to bad cheques. Sentenced to be cashiered.

November 1941   Absconded from the troop ship that was bringing him to England when it docked at Durban in South Africa. Went to Johannesburg where he passed himself off as Captain Selway M.C. of the Argyll and Sutherland Highlanders.

December 1941   Enlisted in South African Air Force under the name of Armstrong. Commissioned, and later promoted to the rank of captain.

May 1944   Seconded to the Royal Air Force. Shot down on the Dutch–German border while piloting a Mitchell bomber.

August 1945   Court-martialled and dismissed from the service in South Africa on six charges, three of conduct prejudicial to good order and military discipline, and three of wearing military decorations without authority.

December 1945   His wealthy South African wife, mother of his only son, divorced him on the grounds of desertion. He is accused, but not charged, with trying to blackmail his ex-wife's family.

February 1946   Arrived back in Britain.

April 1946   Fined at Wimbledon Magistrates Court in south London for wearing a military uniform and decorations to which he was not entitled.

May 1946   Bound and flogged an unidentified woman in a hotel in London's Strand.

June 1946   Murdered Margery Gardner.

July 1946   Murdered Doreen Marshall.

Although Heath was charged with both murders, he was only tried at London's Old Bailey for one. No ex-wife, former girlfriend, or any kind relative was called upon to give evidence on his behalf – and that was the way he wanted it. The defence did not put him in the witness box to give evidence. They knew the arrogant braggart would only dig his own grave if given half a chance to speak for himself. The defence's only chance of getting him off was an insanity verdict. But there was little hope of that . . . given Heath's background.

Two prison doctors testifying for the Crown announced that Heath was indeed a most abnormal person, a sadist, a sexual pervert and a psychopath, but although he had behaved in that most extraordinary way he was not insane.

The court was at a loss to understand what had triggered the sadistic, murderous rage that turned a petty criminal into a predatory vampire. The only common denominator in both murders was that Heath might have been under the influence of alcohol when his depraved passions boiled over – as evidenced by the cabbie who saw him with Margery Gardner, and the night porter who saw him leave with Doreen Marshall.

Heath's counsel, Mr J.D. Casswell, tried in vain to argue that Heath, despite his debonair manner and cool detachment, was mad. Why else would he have written to the police, telephoned the police, gone to the police station voluntarily? He might have known what he was doing, argued Mr Casswell, but he did not know that what he was doing was wrong.

After only one hour's deliberation, the jury found Heath guilty of murder – curiously it was the murder of Margery Gardner, which was more of an accidental death by misadventure than the cold-blooded slaying of Doreen Marshall.

Heath played the role of the debonair playboy to the very end. In what he obviously hoped would be construed as a last noble and gallant gesture in his favour, he requested that all his diaries and address books containing names and details of his womanizing over the years be destroyed before his execution, telling his lawyers, 'I have caused enough trouble in this world without causing more.'

Then, a few days before he was hanged on 26 October 1946, he penned the following words to his mother: 'My only regret about leaving this world is that I've been so damned unworthy of you.'

On the eve of his execution, he again wrote to his mother: 'I shall probably stay up reading tonight because I would like to see the dawn again. So much in my memory is associated with the dawn – early morning patrols and coming home from nightclubs.

'Well, it wasn't a bad life while it lasted. Please don't mourn my going. I would hate that. And please don't wear black.'

When the governor of London's Pentonville Prison and England's most famous hangman, the late Albert Pierrepoint, went to Heath's cell to ask if he had any last requests, the playboy-vampire asked if he could have a whisky. Then, after a few seconds' hesitation, he added: 'On reflection, you might make that a double.'

JOHN GEORGE HAIGH

Acid bath vampire cursed
with lust for blood

After bludgeoning his victims to death, vampire killer John George Haigh drank a glass of their blood before disposing of their bodies in a vat of acid.

'How can you prove murder if there is no body?' he cockily asked Scotland Yard detectives shortly before his arrest for slaying an elderly widow, Mrs Olivia Durand-Deacon, who disappeared from her London hotel in February 1949.

Incredibly, Haigh was so cocksure his murderous plans were foolproof that he, as a self-proclaimed family friend, was the one who actually went to Chelsea police station with another friend of Mrs Durand-Deacon, a woman called Mrs Constance Lane, to report the disappearance of their friend from her lodgings at the respectable, sedate Onslow Court Hotel.

It was then that Haigh's devious web of deceit and dishonesty began unravelling because the female officer on duty, Woman Police Sergeant Audrey Lambourne, was not as gullible as other women who had fallen for Haigh's glib charm.

She was suspicious of the smooth-talking charmer, and reported her gut instinct to her superiors. Officer Lambourne showed remarkable feminine intuition when she explained to Detective Inspector Shelley Symes: 'Apart from the fact that I don't like this man Haigh and his mannerisms, I have a sense that he is "wrong" and there may be a whole different case besides this disappearance.'

Acting on her hunch, senior detectives in turn became even more suspicious when they discovered that the well-dressed, well-spoken man with the neat moustache was an ex-con with an arrest record for swindling. Their suspicions turned to feelings of concern and anguish when Haigh volunteered the information that Mrs Durand-Deacon was supposed to meet him two days earlier at his place of business – but had failed to show up for the appointment.

Back at the Onslow Court Hotel, where Haigh also resided, the cocky little businessman met with crime reporters who were probing Mrs Durand-Deacon's disappearance. He coolly presided over an impromptu press conference at which he told them the same story he had given at the police station. But everyone was suspicious of his obviously exaggerated, agitated concern for the well-being of his friend Mrs Durand-Deacon.

Even as he was holding court with reporters, investigators were focusing their inquiries on Haigh's 'place of business' – a seedy little two-storey brick warehouse-cum-workshop in Leopold Road, Crawley, Sussex, which he leased from a company called Hurtslea Products. Chelsea police had been in touch with the West Sussex Constabulary and their detectives were meticulously going over the premises where Haigh claimed he did 'experimental engineering work'.

There they discovered a gun and a receipt for Mrs Durand-Deacon's expensive Persian lamb coat which had apparently been deposited by Haigh at a local cleaning establishment. The detectives also found out that jewellery items belonging to the missing woman had been sold by Haigh to a jeweller in the neighbouring town of Horsham.

Interviewed at the police station by Detective Inspector Webb, Haigh began by playing a coy cat-and-mouse game with the officer. At first he simply lied, denying all knowledge of the whereabouts of the missing woman. But he began to sweat a little as a .38 Webley revolver, ammunition, a cleaner's ticket for the fur coat, and some of the recovered jewellery were placed in front of him.

'Tell me frankly, what are the chances of convicted murderers ever being released from Broadmoor, the asylum for the criminally insane?' he cryptically asked Inspector Webb.

When the detective gave a noncommittal reply, Haigh became more forthcoming. 'If I told you the truth you wouldn't believe me. It sounds too fantastic for belief,' he went on. 'Mrs Durand-Deacon no longer exists . . . and no trace of her can ever be found again. I have destroyed her with acid!'

Then he gazed long and hard at the interviewing detective, an enigmatic smile on his meek, cherubic face,

99

and asked: 'And how can you prove a murder if there's no body?'

Like other killers before him, Haigh fancied himself as a prison lawyer. He laboured under the false assumption that if there was no body, there was no crime. And, therefore, it could never be proved he was a killer. But the smug vampire was to become buried, not only by his own boasts, but by a flood of incriminating circumstantial evidence.

Meantime, under a false sense of security, he volunteered even more information. 'You'll find what remains of her in the sludge at Leopold Road,' he said of Mrs Durand-Deacon.

His tongue now loosened, he also blurted out to police, 'And I did the same with the Hendersons and the McSwanns', two other luckless families who had been suckered into doing business with the fiendish Haigh.

When he started to realize that the absence of his victims' corpses would not necessarily save him from the gallows, Haigh began telling the detectives that he was a vampire, hoping that his blood-drinking fetish would be construed as insanity. Blood, not money, was his motive, he told amazed detectives. After each killing, he enjoyed nothing more than filling a glass with his victim's blood and draining it to satisfy his insatiable thirst. From what he was telling police, Haigh was one of those rare vampire killers who could quaff large quantities of blood – a known emetic – without becoming physically sick!

Investigators probing Haigh's background, however, came to the conclusion that Haigh was placing too much emphasis on the blood-drinking side of his perverted personality. They tagged him as a petty thief who had spent too much time in prison for theft, and who had come to the conclusion that the only way to escape jail was to make sure there was no one around to testify against him.

During one stretch in prison, he had come up with a fiendish plan to make his victims vanish from the face of the earth: he would melt their bodies in acid. To prove his plan would work he experimented in prison – catching mice, killing them, then dissolving their tiny remains to nothing in metal dishes of powerful acid.

His murderous mission began in earnest shortly after he came out of prison in 1943, when he met Donald McSwann, the son of a former employer. Under the pretence of repairing equipment for his victim, he lured McSwann, a man in his thirties, to a basement workshop he rented in London's Gloucester Road. There he bludgeoned McSwann to death, robbed him of his personal belongings and drank his blood, before dissolving his body in a vat of concentrated sulphuric acid. The melted remains he poured down a drain.

It wasn't long before McSwann's elderly parents came looking for their son. Haigh told them that Donald was out of town on business. Then, a few months later, he lured Mr and Mrs McSwann to his basement chamber of horrors. They too were disposed of in the same macabre fashion. Haigh forged their names on a number of legal documents so he could dispose of the McSwann family's personal property – to the tune of a modest £4,000.

Then it was the Hendersons' turn. Under the pretext of buying property from them, Haigh befriended Dr

Archie Henderson and his wife Rose.

On 12 February 1948 – almost exactly a year prior to Mrs Durand-Deacon's disappearance – he visited Archie Henderson at the Metropole Hotel in Brighton where the Hendersons were staying, and persuaded the retired doctor to come to visit his new business location in Crawley. Cruelly, he battered his new friend to death. Then he drove back to the seaside hotel to collect Rose, telling her that her husband had been taken ill. Anxiously, the poor woman accompanied Haigh to his hellish den in Sussex where she met with the same fate.

Again, Haigh claimed he had drunk their blood before depositing and dissolving their bodies in large drums of sulphuric acid.

After the slayings, Haigh bought himself time by forging letters to friends and relatives of the murdered couple telling them that the Hendersons were going through marital difficulties and had decided to leave the country separately and do a bit of travelling to give their domestic problems time to heal. Then he proceeded to forge letters and documents allowing him to dispose of their property, netting himself a tidy sum.

An inveterate gambler and general wastrel, he had gone through his ill-gotten gains within a year. By 1949, he was overdrawn at the bank and unable to meet his constantly mounting hotel bills.

That February John Haigh was staying at the Onslow Court Hotel, where full-time residents knew him as a personable, successful young business executive who had a pleasant word for everyone. The elderly ladies at the hotel treated him warmly, like a polite favourite nephew.

At the Onslow Court, he sized up fellow-guest Mrs Durand-Deacon as his sixth victim. He struck up a conversation with the sixty-nine-year-old well-to-do widow of a retired army colonel in the hotel dining-room. She was impressed by the well-mannered Haigh, thirty years her junior, who was a regular at the adjacent table in the dining-room. He introduced himself to her as a businessman, and an engineer, with an excellent track record for patenting lucrative inventions.

Mrs Durand-Deacon, who also fancied herself as an inventor, told her new friend that she had an idea about producing artificial fingernails made of plastic. He convinced her that her idea was a potential gold mine and that he could make her dream a reality by manufacturing the plastic fingernails for her. He quickly persuaded her that they should become partners in the venture.

On 18 February 1949, she made a fateful trip to look over their manufacturing plant, the brick warehouse in Crawley – and was never to be seen again.

All that remained of Mrs Durand-Deacon was discovered by Scotland Yard's crack forensic scientist, Professor Keith Simpson. At first Dr Simpson explained to the police that if what Haigh had told them about his acid bath scheme was true there was little chance of any physical evidence of the corpse ever being discovered. Nevertheless, the scientist painstakingly sifted through a patch of sludge – over an area of six feet by four feet and three inches deep – poured carelessly on the ground just outside the workshop.

'Aha! Gallstones!' cried Dr Simpson excitedly as he spotted three small pebbles, each about the size of a cherry, among the muddy sludge.

Immediately, the police shovelled the sludge into a number of containers so it could be taken to Scotland Yard's laboratory for a more extensive examination. There, the sludge was poured like molasses into steel trays and Dr Simpson and his expert team of assistants went to work, using steel surgical probes and extra-strength gloves to protect themselves from the powerful acid residue.

More of Mrs Durand-Deacon came to light than initially expected – certainly enough to send John George Haigh to the scaffold.

The grisly contents of the containers were soon item-ized: a partially dissolved left foot, upper and lower plastic dentures, eighteen fragments of human bone, twenty-eight pounds of a fatty substance, the handle of a red plastic handbag, a lipstick container, and the three cherry-size gallstones.

Dr Simpson took some of the bone fragments to his private laboratory in London's Guy's Hospital for further testing. Incredibly, the top forensic sleuth was able to determine the bones came from a person who suffered from osteo-arthritis in the joints – an ailment which medical records showed plagued Mrs Durand-Deacon.

Police were able to make a plaster cast of the partially dissolved left foot. It matched Mrs Durand-Deacon's shoe size exactly. The handle of the red plastic handbag was identified as belonging to a bag carried by Mrs

Durand-Deacon on the date of her disappearance. The dentures were taken to the unfortunate widow's dentist who had no problem in recalling that these were the dentures he had prescribed for Mrs Durand-Deacon two years earlier. Like the gallstones and the plastic bag handle the plastic dentures were too strongly textured to dissolve in sulphuric acid. In his deadly, supposedly foolproof scheme, this had been overlooked by the devious Mr Haigh. And they were to be used as deadly evidence against him.

Forensic technicians also scraped the recently scrubbed walls and floors of the Crawley warehouse and found traces of human blood. Similar blood samples were found on the dead woman's Persian lamb coat and on the cuff of one of Haigh's shirts.

Haigh's big mouth had helped build a strong case against him. At his trial, Dr Simpson conceded that if Haigh had not bragged about the acid treatment, the clues found in the sludge could have deteriorated to nothing over a period of time, leaving little to indicate the identity of the victim.

Confronted with all this evidence, Haigh volunteered a fuller statement to police in which he described driving Mrs Durand-Deacon from their London hotel to the Crawley warehouse. 'She was inveigled into going to Crawley by me in view of her interest in artificial fingernails. Having taken her into the storeroom at Leopold Road, I shot her in the back of the head while she was examining some paper for use as fingernails.

'Then I went out to the car and fetched in a drinking glass. I made an incision, I think with a pen-knife, at the side of her throat. I collected a glass of blood which I then drank.

'Following that, I removed the coat she was wearing, a Persian lamb fur, and the jewellery, rings, necklace, earrings, and cruciform, and put her in a forty-five gallon tank. Before I put her handbag in the tank, I took cash and her fountain pen from it and kept these. I tipped the rest into the tank with the bag. I filled the tank up with sulphuric acid, by means of a stirrup pump, and left it to react.

'I should have said that in between having her in the tank and pumping in the acid I went round to Ye Olde Ancient Prior's restaurant for a cup of tea and a poached egg on toast.'

Later that evening, after pumping in the acid, police discovered Haigh had gone to the George Hotel in Crawley and treated himself to a three-course dinner which he had eaten heartily as if he hadn't a care in the world. Then he drove back to London and the Onslow Court Hotel.

The only thing about Haigh's statement police were sceptical about was how he had managed to lift and cram Mrs Durand-Deacon's dead body into a four-foot high drum. Haigh was a slightly built young man of about 135 pounds, Mrs Durand-Deacon a buxom lady at least fifty pounds heavier.

Haigh, almost pleased with himself, was only too eager to explain, in this cold and dispassionate addition to his statement. 'I laid the barrel on its side on the floor and, with the minimum of effort, pushed her head and shoulders in. I then tipped the barrel up by placing my feet on the forward edge and grasping the top of the barrel with my gloved hands.

'By throwing my weight backwards the barrel containing the body rocked to a vertical position fairly easily. I found that I could raise a 185-pound body very easily. You might think that a 45-gallon drum only four feet high would be too small for such a body. But my experiments showed that as the drum tipped, the body slumped down to the shoulders and the legs disappeared below the surface of the drum.'

Haigh confessed that a couple of days prior to his arrest he had made another trip to Crawley to see how Mrs Durand-Deacon's body was decomposing. The process did not appear to be going fast enough, so the callous killer added more acid to the drum. In a subsequent, final visit he emptied the drum's sludge contents outside the brick storeroom.

As the horrible facts of the case were made public, the London newspapers had a field day. Headlines shouted the arrest of a genuine 'Modern-day Vampire' and 'The Story of a Vampire Killer'. In fact, the sensational tabloids got carried away with the lurid nature of the Haigh case. One of them, the *Daily Mirror*, went so far as to publish information which the Crown considered prejudicial to the fairness of the upcoming trial.

'Vampire – a Man Held' screamed the *Mirror's* front-page headline on the morning of 4 March 1949, followed by a story beginning: 'The Vampire Killer will never strike again. He is safely behind bars, powerless to lure victims to a hideous death.'

The Director of Public Prosecutions was not amused.

In a country where the law stresses an accused's innocence until he is found guilty, and frowns on crucial
details of a murder investigation being made public prior
to a trial, the *Daily Mirror's* approach to the story was
audacious and legally challenging. The paper's over-
enthusiastic editor, Sylvester Bolam, was sentenced to
three months' imprisonment for contempt of court.

Awaiting trial in prison, Haigh continued to revel in
his notoriety as a modern-day vampire, relishing the
garish publicity. He had found fame at last! And indeed
he did everything he could to reinforce the perverse
public image of himself.

He claimed that he was not a predator who killed
simply for money. There was some basis in fact for this
contention by Haigh. In his five years as a killer, his
murders did not net him more than £9,600 all told, which
included the pitiful £110 he got for Mrs Durand-
Deacon's coat and jewellery. To bolster his claim that
money was not a factor, Haigh told psychiatrists there
were three other victims that the police did not know
about – three penniless unfortunates whom he had lured
to his lair over a three-year period and killed purely and
simply for the thrill of drinking their blood.

One victim was a London woman in her thirties; the
second was a man called Max, also in his thirties, whom
he had met casually in a London pub; and the third was a
Welsh girl called Mary, whom he had met in the coastal
resort of Eastbourne. All three he had bludgeoned to
death for the sole purpose of draining and drinking their
blood. But police could not come up with any evidence
that these sacrificial blood victims ever existed anywhere

but in Haigh's vivid, perverted fantasies.

Haigh's background did not conform to that of a kinky vampire sadist. Born in working-class Yorkshire, the only son of a miner, he came from a deeply religious background and had a strict God-fearing upbringing. He was never an unhappy child, and his parents took pride in the fact he always kept himself clean, neat, and smart-looking. Although not a great scholar, he was well-liked at school where he once won a prize for writing a particularly sensitive religious essay. A music lover, he sang with the prestigious Wakefield Cathedral choir at the age of twelve, and was a talented pianist. If he had one fault, it was a tendency to tell lies.

At twenty-one he left home to make his own way in the world. He desperately wanted to become an auto engineer, but his ambition overtook his education and talent in this field.

He married, but soon got into financial straits. As a direct result, he got involved in an automobile credit scam 'to make fast, easy money'. This earned him the first of three prison terms, and while he was in jail his new bride deserted him.

Explaining why he turned to a life of crime, he justified himself later when he wrote to a friend: 'When I first discovered there were easier ways of making money than by working long hours in an office, I did not ask myself if what I was doing was right or wrong. That seemed to me to be irrelevant.'

In 1936, he went to London where he diligently followed his chosen path of crime, earning himself two more prison stretches for his efforts.

In the early wartime years, he worked as a fire-watcher during the carnage and horror of the Blitz which, he claimed later, alienated him totally from God and religion.

It was during this period, Haigh told prison doctors, that he became cursed with the lust for blood, after a road accident when his car overturned after colliding with a truck. When he regained consciousness after the crash, he couldn't see and instinctively put his hand to his face. To his horror, his face was a bloody mess . . . blood poured down over his eyes and into his mouth. Since then he had been haunted by recurring dreams of a forest of crucifixes which turned into trees dripping with blood.

In a chilling diary, vampire Haigh described his horribly graphic fantasies: 'In my dream I see before me a forest of crucifixes which gradually turn into trees. At first there appears to be dew or rain dripping from the branches, but as I approach I realize it is blood. Suddenly the whole forest begins to writhe. The trees, stark and erect, ooze blood. A man goes to each tree catching the blood in a cup. When his cup is full he approaches me. "Drink," he says. But I am unable to move.'

Mysterious voices still urged him to drink blood, he told psychiatrists. Under close observation while in jail, the weird Mr Haigh was witnessed on a number of occasions drinking his own urine.

A battery of ten psychiatrists, however, agreed – with one exception – that the prisoner was a sane, though diabolical schemer. Only Dr Henry Yellowlees, for the defence, argued that Haigh was genuinely paranoid.

Nor did a jury buy Haigh's bizarre tales of paranoid delusions. At his trial which began at Lewes Assizes on 18 July 1949, the jury agreed with the psychiatrists' evaluation that Haigh was a calculating killer feigning insanity. It took them only seventeen minutes to return a guilty verdict.

Asked if he had anything to say, Haigh responded simply, 'Nothing at all.'

He did open up a bit more prior to his execution when he penned a brief autobiography for the Sunday tabloid, *News of the World*. Haigh hinted that his strict religious upbringing – as a member of the puritanically rigid Plymouth Brethren sect – might have had something to do with his straying from the moral path.

Haigh, an only child, wrote:

Although my parents were kind and loving, I had none of the joys or companionship young children usually have.

From my earliest years I have recollections of my father saying, 'Do not', or 'Thou shalt not'. Any form of entertainment or sport was frowned upon and not regarded as edifying. My parents' attitude was usually one of condemnation and prohibition.

It is true to say that I was nurtured on Bible stories. But these stories were mostly concerned with sacrifice. If I ever did anything which my father regarded as improper, he would say, 'Do not grieve the Lord by behaving so.' And if I suggested I wanted to go out somewhere, or go to meet somebody, my father would say, 'No, it would not please the Lord.'

My father told me that my mother was an angel, but that he was a sinner.

Haigh also recounted how his father had built a high wall around their modest home to keep the powers of Satan and other evils at bay.

Haigh's father worked in a coal mine and had been injured on the forehead by a piece of flying coal. It had left a vivid blue scar. 'He told me that it was the mark that Satan put on sinners, and that I would be marked in blue like that if I sinned.

'Each night before I fell asleep I would run my fingers across my forehead wondering all the time when I was going to get cursed with that blue brand of Satan,' remembered the self-proclaimed vampire on the eve of his execution.

Haigh was hanged at Wandsworth Prison on 6 August, 1949.

ANDREI CHIKATILO

Incredible reign of terror
of Russian cannibal-vampire

Rostov, Russia   With his shaved bald head and wild eyes, Andrei Chikatilo looked for all the world like Nosferatu, the monster from the original silent-movie version of *Dracula*, as he glared menacingly from behind his barred cage in a Russian courtroom. 'I am a freak of nature . . . a mad beast,' the fifty-six-year-old former schoolteacher and graduate of Rostov University said chillingly as he confessed to killing at least fifty-three people, mostly schoolchildren, between 1978 and 1990, drinking their blood and cannibalizing them.

Victims' relatives in court swooned and one was taken to hospital as they heard that Chikatilo's twelve-year reign of terror was primarily the result of botched police work in this city of 1.4 million citizens 600 miles south of Moscow – due mainly to lack of publicity about a monster on the loose, and a lack of communication between police departments.

Crime was seldom publicized in the pre-glasnost

Soviet Union when Chikatilo embarked on his spine-chilling murder spree in the late 1970s. As a result, almost five years elapsed before Rostov residents were alerted to the fact that one of the world's worst serial killers was operating in their midst. More than 200,000 people were questioned and blood-tested during the decade-long investigation. An innocent man named Alexander Kravchenko was arrested, convicted and put to death in 1978 for the brutal killing of a nine-year-old girl whom Chikatilo later confessed had been his first victim. Another man arrested and falsely accused of the crimes during the investigation committed suicide. A third wrongfully accused citizen made an unsuccessful attempt to kill himself. Amazingly, Chikatilo was taken in for questioning twice during that period, but released because of inconclusive blood and semen tests.

In a remarkable piece of psychological detection at the height of the savage killing spree, prominent psychiatrist Dr Aleksandr Bukhanovsky was asked to draw up a profile of the possible perpetrator. With unerring accuracy, Bukhanovsky described a middle-aged man with an especially cruel childhood, a terrible inferiority complex, and with serious sexual problems. He added that the killer was heterosexual, probably married, and had at one time possibly been a schoolteacher.

Throughout the murderous reign which began when he was forty-two years old, Chikatilo maintained a remarkable double life. He was married with children, a pillar of the local Communist party, and worked as a Russian language teacher as well as at other white-collar jobs.

Chikatilo was arrested when a police officer, watching a bus stop on a massive surveillance operation, saw a young schoolboy following a lanky, bespectacled middle-aged man. Chikatilo refused to say anything to his interrogators for nine defiant days. He only broke down and confessed after Dr Bukhanovsky's amazingly accurate profile was read to him.

Then he began to tell police about a traumatic incident in his life when his older brother was killed and eaten by starving peasants in the Ukraine during a famine in the 1930s, how his father was a prisoner-of-war who was treated like a traitor when he returned home, how he felt inadequate with women – although he had married and had two children – and how he had been mocked and humiliated for the best part of his life. He blamed the injustices of the Soviet system and his own sexual inadequacies for triggering the murdering rages which turned him into a stalking monster.

'I gave myself to my work, my studies, my family, my children and my grandchildren,' confessed the man who had been described as 'the perfect husband'. 'But when I found myself in a different setting, I became a different person, uncontrollable, as if some evil force was controlling me against my will. And I could not resist.'

During Chikatilo's trial, the court heard how he usually found his young victims at bus stops. He would offer them rides in his car, or invite them to visit his nearby cabin – neither car nor cabin existed.

Gullible and innocent schoolchildren would follow him, usually to a wooded area beside a railroad track called Forest Strip (Chikatilo was nicknamed the Forest

Strip Vampire), where he would suddenly pounce, using his knife, hands and teeth as weapons. In a frenzy, he would gouge out their eyes, mutilate vulnerable young bodies, drink blood, and eat body parts – an unspeakable ritual he was to repeat dozens of times. He would then bury his victims in the wooded copse.

Prosecutors could not accept his contention that the pressures of Communism (which he had voluntarily supported), were the trigger for his actions. 'His goal was a sexual act,' said chief investigator Amirkhan Yandiyev. 'And when he tried to rape his victims and found he could not complete the act, then he became sadistic.' The prosecutor said Chikatilo felt no remorse for his victims – only pity for himself.

'He tortured his victims while they were alive by biting out their tongues, tearing away their sexual organs, and cutting their bellies open,' Judge Leonid Akubzhanov wrote in his verdict against Chikatilo.

Chikatilo was found guilty and sentenced to death on 15 October 1992, to be executed in traditional Russian style – a bullet in the back of the head. Victims' relatives tried to storm the courtroom to get to the monster. 'Give him to us. Let us deal with him,' cried bereaved mothers as an indignant Chikatilo was led from his courtroom cage, whining and protesting that he had been given an unfair trial.

'I understand your feelings and your inability to hold yourselves back. I understand. But we must have due process of law,' Judge Akubzhanov tried to pacify the weeping relatives.

Although police were declaring Chikatilo's arrest,

conviction and death sentence a triumph, most Rostov residents – overwhelmed by many now-publicized crime waves accompanying the collapse of the Soviet Union – are not so sure. As the southern Russian newspaper, *Nashye Vremya* pointed out: 'It's not such a triumph to have caught a criminal after leaving him on the loose for twelve years.'

THE CULT VAMPIRE

SEAN RICHARD SELLERS

The model schoolboy who became
a blood-drinking night stalker

Sandy-haired, fresh-faced Sean Sellers was the all-American high-school teenager, excelling at both athletics and academic studies. He also had a flair for melodrama which made him stand out in his high-school acting group. An avid reader who scored straight As, if he wasn't the most popular kid at school, he was certainly one of the most talked about. Schoolmates voted him the most eccentric kid in his class – and the one most likely to become a vampire.

Sean carried his own lunch to school – vials of his blood which he kept refrigerated at home. And at lunch breaks he used to shock his fellow students by quaffing them hungrily.

He never travelled very far without his favourite reading material, the Satanic Bible, under his arm. He never joined any high-school clubs, because he was a member and leader of his own off-the-wall group, a Satanic coven which revelled in clandestine rituals such as blood-drinking – and cold-blooded murder.

Now a twenty-three-year-old, Sean is still a studious type. But these days he whiles away his time reading, writing poetry, and pencilling his chilling memoirs in Oklahoma State Penitentiary – among the youngest of seventy-one savage killers on Death Row. He says he's ready and willing to go to the chair, but his appeals against the death sentence are still tied up in the complex legal system.

He landed in Death Row because of his vampirish ways and his dedication to the cult of Satan, whom he blames for seducing him into callously shooting three innocent victims – his own mum and stepdad and an innocent shop assistant.

Sellers now says he was driven to kill because of the love-starved childhood which turned him to evil. 'If I had had a close family relationship, I might not have got into Satanism,' he says, by way of trying to mitigate his callous deeds. 'There was an absence, and Satan filled that.'

At his trial he displayed the same unemotional self-denial. He entered pleas of not guilty to three counts of first-degree murder, swearing he had absolutely no recollection of committing the meticulously planned executions. If he carried them out, argued his lawyers, he must have been insane at the time – an impressionable innocent possessed by Satan, and subject to his evil master's every whim.

Finding him guilty of all three slayings, the jury saw it differently. 'We thought he knew right from wrong,' said one juror. Another added: 'If our verdict saves one kid from Satanism, or saves one other person from getting killed, then it is justified.'

As Sean Sellers sits on Death Row awaiting execution in the electric chair, he says he is no longer a Satanic devotee. His converstion has gone full circle. He has become a born-again Christian, he claims.

He has also become a media star and isn't shy about appearing by satellite on television talk shows to warn about the dangers of Satanic cults. He explains his current crusade thus: 'I'm having a hard time dealing with the guilt, but I have to tell the truth about what Satanism can do.'

As Sean tells it, his troubles go all the way back to 1972 when his attractive blonde mother Vonda, who was only fifteen when she got married, divorced Sean's natural father, artist Jason Sellers, and was forced to leave her bright three-year-old son in the care of a succession of relatives while she travelled around the country seeking work.

Four years later, Vonda, now twenty-one, was re-married to a hard-working, conscientious former Green Beret recruiting sergeant and Vietnam vet, Paul Leon Bellofatto, a mechanic eleven years her senior. Bellofatto readily adopted the role of stepdad, accepting Sean as his own. But in these early years, they were never exactly a stable family unit. To make big money fast, Vonda and new husband Lee – as Paul Bellofatto was better known – became a husband and wife long-distance truck-driving team which meant prolonged absences from their precocious and impressionable seven-year-old son.

Alternately, Sean became the charge of Vonda's parents, Jim and Geneva Blackwell, or her sister, Debbie Crenshaw, who says today: 'I think he resented his mother from the time he was little because she left him alone.'

Grandfather Jim Blackwell recalls that Vonda and Lee were always pretty strict with Sean – even relaying decisions and orders about his life when they were on the road. 'They thought Sean was never good enough. They demanded more from him than any kid could give. He was a timid, beaten-down kid who had a need to be accepted. I can look back now and see where he was susceptible to anything.'

However, the adolescent Sean was able to use his natural acting abilities to conceal his painful feelings of rejection. Although he was bounced from town to town and school to school, his education was never neglected. Indeed he was an extremely fast-learning student. Reading was his passion, particularly action and adventure stories and tales of mind-boggling science fiction. Too young to have a library card, he persuaded a babysitter to check out more esoteric books from public libraries for him to read to satisfy his insatiable curiosity. These books were invariably about the occult and the supernatural . . . and he was soon to develop a taste for books dealing with the dark side of life, including Satanism.

His young mind aflame with fantasy, at the age of twelve he became fascinated with the controversial game Dungeons and Dragons, an activity replete with scenarios of death and intrigue which has been widely criticized as a mind-bending recreation responsible for other teen-age tragedies.

Later, at Sean's trial, one of the witnesses called by the defence was Patricia Pulling of Richmond, Virginia, president of BADD (Bothered About Dungeons and Dragons). Her teenage son had committed suicide because of his fascination with the morbid game, Mrs Pulling told the court. In all, 100 murders and suicides had been linked to involvement in the game of Dungeons and Dragons.

In fact, it was from the time that he first became interested in the Dungeons and Dragons game that the clean-cut, handsome and intelligent child Sean began to change. From an inquisitive, outwardly normal young-ster he turned into a sullen, introverted pre-teen, and when Vonda and Lee Bellofatto's long-distance trucking business hit a rough patch and they decided to settle down and create a family home and environment that was the different Sean they came back to.

Settling down with his mother and stepfather in a suburb of Oklahoma City, Sean was able to ally himself with his first real friend, a youth called Richard Howard who had also been raised by grandparents and who shared Sean's passion for the game Dungeons and Dragons. The boys were inseparable, and both were members of the football, track and weight-lifting teams at junior high school.

However, it wasn't long before the Bellofatto family uprooted again, this time transplanting themselves to Greeley, Colorado, where, in the summer of 1983, Lee had found himself a new job.

Sean was sullen about losing his friend Richard. But his spirits rose when he found himself a girlfriend at Greeley, a young lass he met at a church camp. The teenage romance soon turned sour, though. Feeling lovelorn and rejected, Sean contemplated suicide after romance left his life.

Chillingly, his self-pity over puppy love gone wrong turned to bitterness. He began thinking darker thoughts, and he dedicated himself to Satanism. He described his thoughts at that time in his diary: 'I was mad at God. Deep down I want power . . . the power of the supernatural.'

In March of the following year, there was turmoil again in Sean's young life. Vonda and Lee decided to resume their long-distance driving career, so the family left Colorado. Sean was placed in the care of Vonda's sister Debbie who lived in Okmulgee, Oklahoma.

Sean's rebellion began to show. He didn't feel he fitted in at his new high school. He missed Greeley where he had friends who shared his morbid interests, and he went back to see them at every opportunity.

One visit to Greeley was truly memorable for him. Dressed in black and equipped with a silver chalice and a ritual sword, he and a friend presided at the inaugural Satanic baptism of one of their new disciples. They dressed the novice in a white sheet, recalls Sean, then 'we commanded him to strip naked. We cut him and drank his blood. We used the same blood to write a dedication to Satan.'

Sean was delighted when, after a couple of months, his

parents decided to give up the long-distance driving business for good. They returned to Oklahoma City, where Sean was happy to team up again with his old best friend and soulmate Richard Howard. He wasted no time filling Richard in on the excitement of Satanism. Word spread, and the pair managed to find other impressionable teenagers eager to share their dark secrets.

By February 1985, Sean was immersed in Satan worship. In his bedroom at home, he spent hours performing solitary rituals, lighting candles and burning incense. There were occasions when he would slash his own body so he could write messages in his blood to the powers of darkness. One such message left no doubts as to his total conversion to evil: 'I renounce God, I renounce Christ. I will serve only Satan . . . Hail Satan.'

Sean's private thoughts and deeds intruded more and more into his public behaviour. He began playing truant from Putnam City North High School and was no longer the model student. His interest in sports activities vanished. His clean-cut look was abandoned for a new long-haired, dishevelled appearance. He began to wear the left sleeve of his shirts rolled up, and he let the nail on the pinky finger of his left hand grow to become a long, sharp talon. He painted the nail jet black – the symbol of a devil-worshipper. To give himself a more Satanic look he would draw dark circles round his eyes with eye-liner.

Sean's days and nights centred around Satanism. He enjoyed dressing all in black, emulating a Japanese ninja assassin, or for that matter a vampire who liked to stalk his prey under cover of darkness. Skulking about like that in the neighbourhood in the wee hours of the morning, Sellers earned a new nickname among school-mates – 'the night roamer'. He popped amphetamines to fuel his fantasies, and also drank booze and smoked marijuana.

When his stepfather Lee came across Sean's Satanic artefacts stashed in his bedroom he hit the roof. Confis-cating the articles and Sean's morbid reading material, he pointed a finger at his deviant son and snarled furiously: 'You no longer exist!' Lee Bellofatto was one of the few people to see into the evil heart of his stepson, and he seethed inwardly when he saw how the boy's dramatic behavioural transformation was tearing Vonda apart. Lee was never again to have any kind of relation-ship with Sean.

At school, Sean's teachers were equally perturbed. Sean was forever quoting in class from his Satanic Bible, made a big show of drinking blood in the lunch-room, and took delight in spreading his evil Satanic gospel to anyone who would listen. He openly canvassed for potential new Satanic followers in the school corridors and recreation areas.

In a biology class one day, he shocked both the teacher and fellow students when he picked up a live frog, sadistically chomped down on its wriggling leg, and ate it.

His devoted mother Vonda was at her wits' end. She persuaded him to attend a Bible-study group at their local church, where he also received counselling from a local priest. Sean had a one-on-one conversation with a particularly understanding priest, the Rev. John Michaels.

However, it was no problem for a consummate actor like Sean to give the Rev. Michaels a total snow job. The teenager laughed scornfully and flatly denied the allegations that he had serious ties to Satanism. He charmingly disarmed Father Michaels on the subject of his Satanic literature and other paraphernalia. Laughingly, he dismissed his talk about Satan as just his way of 'having fun'. And the sword, chalice and altar, not to mention all these books? 'They're just curiosities to me, but they're my property and I should have them back,' he told the priest who by this time was totally taken in by the intelligent and articulate teenager.

So much for intervention. Everyone assumed the teenager was at the awkward age where kids develop bizarre tastes and interests. 'Humour him, he'll grow out of it,' Vonda was told. And to humour him, Sean's precious Satanic accessories and literature were returned to him.

Despite all the counselling and indulgence, Sean was not to be dissuaded from his path of evil. He took to frequenting occult book stores. At one he met an older woman, a self-proclaimed witch who gave him books which fuelled his already demented fantasies even more. Sean revelled in the bizarre and enjoyed attending regular film screenings of the cult classic movie, *The Rocky Horror Picture Show*. He continued to make more and more friends who shared his morbid beliefs. With Richard and a coterie of half a dozen or so followers, Sean convened regular meetings in an abandoned farmhouse which they converted to a temple of Satanic worship.

'I was like a vampire. We were always cutting each other up and drinking each other's blood,' Sean confessed later. Before long Sean had broken several of the Ten Commandments, and was seeking fresh devilish mischief. After all, there was one important Biblical commandment he hadn't yet broken: 'Thou shalt not kill.'

To pluck up courage to kill with impunity, Sean summoned up a demonic *alter ego* who could commit murder for him – a monstrous entity he called Ezurate who was to fill his mind and being as he embarked on a new fiendish path in his troubled teenage life.

The day selected for the killing was 8 September 1985. Sean's and his friend Richard's versions of the events of that fateful day differ dramatically. Whatever happened, both were in and around the Circle K convenience store when an innocent shop assistant, thirty-six-year-old Robert Bower – who had once refused to sell the under-age youths beer – was viciously gunned down.

As Sean recalls it, Richard stole his grandfather's gun, a .357 Magnum, and they drove to the remotely located convenience store late at night and confronted Bower. They engaged an unsuspecting Bower in conversation. Then when there were no other customers around, Sean pulled out the gun, pointed it at Bower and fired. The first shot missed, smashing a display counter behind the terrified Bower.

Blind with fear, Bower ran aimlessly around the store, knocking over display stands in his desperate panic to escape his cold-eyed merciless assassin. Slowly, Sellers stalked Bower, hitting him in the back of the neck with his second shot. His face a sheet of blood, Bower fell to the floor. Cold-hearted Sellers stood over him, smirking, and placed a final and fatal shot in Bower's writhing body.

Sean laughed crazily as he and Richard fled the murder scene to Howard's grandfather's home where Sellers carefully cleaned the .357 Magnum and returned it to the briefcase from which it had been stolen. Howard's grandfather, a police officer, was only to learn later that his gun, a tool of his trade, had been used as a murder weapon.

Now totally steeped in Satanism, Sean had developed a bloodlust which yearned for more sacrificial victims. His frustration and resentment for his stern parents worsened. They would not allow Sean to go and live with his friend Richard, now a high-school drop-out, and his new wife Tracey. Sean found himself another girlfriend, a fifteen-year-old called Angel. But Vonda and Lee disapproved, and to Sean's chagrin, forbade him to see her. A plan for Sean to go and live with his natural father in California came to nothing.

Sean at first vented his frustration in a classroom essay which shocked his teacher. He wrote, in part: 'Satanism has made me a better person. I am free. I can kill without remorse!'

Alarmed, the teacher called his parents and told Vonda about her son's bizarre essay. The teacher quoted disturbing excerpts from the essay over the phone, including the line: 'I feel no regret or sorrow, only love, hate or joy. Only I may understand, but that is enough – evil has taught me good, good has shown me evil.'

White-faced and horror-struck at the other end of the line, Vonda was chilled to the marrow as she listened to her son's heartless essay. Trembling, she thanked the teacher and hung up. She ran to Sean's bedroom scared of what she would find. The first thing she came across was a journal which Sean had innocently titled 'Diary of Prose'. The diary echoed the same macabre thoughts she had listened to from the boy's school essay. In it, Sean wrote of 'deep problems within me, far too deep to find'. On another page he talked about 'a lover's choice to die by hurling himself off a cliff to be with his girl again'.

Remembering how she and Lee had intervened to forbid Sean from seeing his teenage drop-out girlfriend Angel, Vonda thought the worst: Sean was contemplating suicide. Desperate, the concerned mum tried to communicate with him with some emotional prose of her own.

Weeping, she sat down and wrote Sean a touching letter – a letter he was never to read:

My dearest and most precious son,
I love you very much and would give my life for you without a second thought. Maybe I don't always handle things in a proper manner, but my side of it isn't easy either. Sometimes you and I do better to talk on paper than in person.

The day you were born was the happiest day of my life. I became an over-protective mother – perhaps too over-protective. I cry from frustration because I couldn't protect you from life's plain and simple facts. I still cry sometimes when I'm alone because I feel so helpless to help you.

I struggled to make a living for us, and finally left you and went to driving a truck, not because I wanted to, but because I could make better money so you could have what you wanted and needed. I always wanted to be with you, but I made my choice and have lived with it, however wrong it might have been.

Right now, I see you pressing to be something that I've never seen in my life. But I can't help you unless you talk to me. And if you decide to, be honest with me and I will really try to help.

Sean, to be strong you don't have to put on a tough outside appearance. You, my son, are very strong. But you need to release your pain. Emotions are one of the biggest controlling factors in a person's life. Please don't think it's just because I'm a woman that I'm saying that – Lee will tell you the same thing.

This past summer vacation has been miserable for you. But it's over. Let go of it, son. In fact, you need to let go of several things from the past six months. You are hurting yourself more than you realize. How can I help you? I think maybe too much responsibility has been put on you for you to realize. Be honest with yourself and try to talk. I will listen.

You are a good, honest young man. But you are having problems sorting things out. But unless you let me help, what can I do? I'll always love you no matter what. I'll always be there when you need me, no matter what, until the day I die.

The day of her death was to be that same evening.

Sean never read his mum's touching letter which she left in his bedroom, placed carefully on top of his incriminating 'Diary of Prose'.

Arriving home late from his part-time job in a pizza parlour, Sean went into his bedroom and prepared himself for a night of blood-letting with a particularly elaborate Satanic ritual. First, he stripped naked, then donned the black underpants which he wore for rituals. He draped himself in a long black cape which he had tailored for himself. He lit his candles and incense, poured blood into the silver chalice on his makeshift altar, and invoked his demonic *alter ego* Ezurate.

His unsuspecting parents were sound asleep in the next bedroom. Sean fell asleep himself for a brief period. When he awoke he found his stepfather's .44 revolver. And, with the help of his personal demon Ezurate, steeled himself for an evening of carnage.

The boy in black stealthily made his way to his parents' bedroom, with all the skill of a ninja assassin stalking his prey.

Sean's memory of what happened that night has returned. He dispassionately recalls: 'My heart started beating fast, then everything went calm. I pointed the gun at my dad's head and fired. I pointed the gun at my mum's head and fired.'

There was a little more to it than that. He described

the killings in some detail when questioned by police. Both Vonda and Lee were sleeping on their stomachs. The first shot was aimed at stepdad Lee. He was blasted in the back of the head and died instantly. Then he fired at the back of Vonda's head. Blood seeped through her long blonde hair, soaking the pillow. But shot two didn't kill her. Blinded with blood, she struggled to raise herself into a sitting position in bed.

We will never know whether or not, in these few fleeting seconds before death, she recognized her killer as the cherished son she had vowed to lay down her life for only a few hours earlier. Sean mercilessly pulled the trigger again at pointblank range. Vonda died.

After the vicious slaughter. Sean calmly and methodically covered his tracks to make the killings look like the work of a burglar. After all, he hadn't committed the atrocious deed, it was the work of his *alter ego*, the demon Ezurate. It wasn't Ezurate, though, but Sean who put the carefully thought out alibi plan into action. As his parents' corpses lay only yards away, Sean stripped and showered to wash away his mother's last drops of blood which had spattered his face and neck.

After a thorough scrub down, he went into his bedroom and carefully put away his Satanic symbols, ritual sword and chalice. Then he went around the house, opening dresser drawers to give the appearance that the home had been ransacked by burglars. He unlatched and slid open a glass sliding patio door to make it look as if that was how the intruders gained entry.

Then he drove in his white pick-up truck to his friend Richard's house. He told Richard what he had done, and

135

tried to persuade Howard and his wife to provide him with the alibi that he had spent the entire night at their house after finishing work at the pizza parlour. At Sean's urging, Howard hid the .44 Smith & Wesson in an air vent, but later wrapped the revolver in a towel, concealed it in a used pizza carton and put it out in the rubbish.

As for Sean, he went to bed and slept like a baby.

The next morning Sean exulted as he went back to his home with his friend Richard. While Howard and his wife – whom he had by now persuaded to be his 'alibi' witnesses – waited outside, Sean went in to review his grisly handiwork, taking delight in the irony that he was to be the one to 'discover' the murders. With his gift for the dramatic, he ran screaming to a neighbour's house to call an ambulance, crying all the time: 'There's all this blood!'

But Sean wasn't fooling many people for long, particularly those relatives who knew him best. His aunt Debbie recalls her immediate reaction: 'We all had the same instinct. We had a feeling he had done it.'

Grandfather Jim Blackwell too was well aware that there had been big trouble between Vonda and Lee and Sean. His daughter had called him regularly to confide in him about Sean's bizarre behaviour. Mr Blackwell knew in his heart of hearts that his grandson was the merciless killer of his daughter. Thus it was with a heavy heart that he drove to the police station to talk to the officer in charge of the murder investigation, Detective Ron Mitchell.

'Do you have any idea who killed them?' Blackwell asked the detective.

The police, suspicious of the way the crime scene was set up, were already convinced they were dealing with an inside job. 'We have people we want to question some more,' the detective told the grieving grandfather.

'Someone close to home?'

'Yes.'

Blackwell fell silent for a few moments. 'I was afraid you were going to say that,' he sighed resignedly.

His gut feeling was right. Young Sean was the one who had brutally murdered his daughter. Blackwell's immediate reaction was that the killing spree, if indeed one had begun, had to be stopped. He knew his grandson could be a difficult nut to crack, and advised Detective Mitchell to focus the next step of his investigation on Sean's buddy and key alibi witness, Richard Howard.

Howard, when called for a second round of questions, was easily persuaded to tell everything he knew about the death of Sean's parents and the whereabouts of the hidden murder weapon. And when pressed, he also spilled the beans about the slaying of the shop assistant Robert Bower six months earlier.

When arrested, Sean's immediate defence was that he could not recall committing any of the killings. After that bald statement he remained silent, except for one period when he sobbed uncontrollably to detectives: 'If I killed them, I don't know it.' He did not talk much at all after he was charged, and at his trial the defence elected not to put him on the stand to testify on his own behalf. But as his mum's touching letter was later read out in court, he sobbed again: 'I loved my parents!'

His friend Richard was originally charged with murder for his part in the Bower shooting. Howard insisted that it was Sellers who had stolen his grandfather's gun, that he was outside the Circle K store at the time of the shooting, and knew nothing about the slaying until Sean told him about it. A key witness in the prosecution's case against Sellers, Howard pleaded guilty to being an accessory after the fact and received a deferred sentence of five years.

Now that his memory has come back, media star Sean Sellers seems resigned to his death by execution. He tells visitors: 'I thought I would go free at first because I didn't think I was guilty. Then when I got the death penalty I wanted to know why. I kept meditating and thinking, going back in time and then forward again. When I hit a blank spot, I forced myself to remember. I think now I was two people – Sean and Ezurate.'

In a telephone interview from his jail cell, Sellers did not want to talk about his criminal acts. He preferred to dwell more on his religious rebirth. He does, however, speak out against Satanism and how it got him in a vice-like grip.

Of the events leading up to the killings, he recalls: 'I started having dreams, and the dreams are what really influenced me. I wasn't getting much sleep at the time. But when I did dream, the dreams I was having were sick dreams, full of blood, stuff much worse than the *Friday the 13th*-type movies.'

Detectives on the murder investigative team are not only cynical about Sean's preoccupation about being reborn, they are also highly sceptical about the role Satanism played in the homicides. Most of them feel Sellers was just an evil young thrill-killer. He committed his crimes out of hate, for kicks, and without remorse. 'Satanism was not the cause,' commented Detective Robert Jones. 'That was just another symptom of his twisted little mind. He was a pseudo-Satan worshipper . . . he was full of bull.'

Meantime, erstwhile vampire turned born-again Christian Sellers added: 'Now that I remember all of this, of course I want to die. But the Lord has given me a burden to reach out and help other people . . . so no one else will follow in my footsteps.'

MAGDALENA SOLIS

High priestess of
blood-drinking sex cult

Magdalena Solis had a chequered career – Monterey,
Mexico, prostitute . . . lesbian . . . and high priestess of
her own blood-drinking sex cult.

Magdalena and her brother Eleazor – who also dou-
bled as her pimp – were recruited by two evil cultists to
pose as mystical gods so the gang could extort money
and sex from their gullible followers. The perverted plan
was the brainchild of brothers Santos and Cayetano
Hernandez.

In the early weeks of 1963, the diabolical, sex-
obsessed Hernandez brothers managed to convince the
inhabitants in and around the remote village of Yerba
Buena in the state of Taumaulipas (incidentally the same
province that saw the birth and carnage of the infamous
Adolfo de Jesus Constanzo blood-drinking, drug-
smuggling cult) that the Inca gods of the mountain were
willing to give them fabulous wealth and treasure in
exchange for their undivided loyalty and sexual favours.

The ignorant peasant-folk were open to any suggestion. They did not give a thought to the fact that the Incas were of Peruvian origin, and that if they did have any mountain gods, they would more probably be Aztecs. Why they swallowed the Hernandez' promises hook, line and sinker, to this day remains a mystery of the mountains.

Yet equally inexplicable in American culture is the blind devotion which prompted young middle-American men and women to commit senseless slaughters in the name of the Charles Manson Family. And who can ever forget the lemming syndrome as it struck in Jonestown, Guyana, where close to 900 Peoples' Temple disciples keeled over in a mass suicide at the instigation of their leader Jim Jones?

Incredibly, the Hernandez scam worked like a dream. The gullible villagers cleaned out caves in the mountainside overlooking the village to be used as temples for elaborate, but meaningless, rituals dreamed up by the two Hernandez brothers.

For months, the womenfolk of the poor village of peasants gladly offered their bodies to Santos Hernandez, convinced that their sexual sacrifices would please the gods and bring them good fortune. In the case of Cayetano Hernandez, a homosexual, the men and young boys of the village yielded willingly to his perverted sexual desires in the hope of a spiritual windfall.

However, even the most ignorant among them became suspicious after three months of trying to trade sex for good fortune. No gods ever appeared or sent them messages of thanks for their sexual sacrifices. Nor were there any visible signs of improvement in their fortunes or hard-working lifestyles.

The Hernandez brothers realized that they had to do some quick-thinking. They were being treated royally by the villagers and the freewheeling sex was more than they could handle, but they were in danger of seeing their devious scheme going down the drain. So to satisfy some disgruntled and muttering customers, the sly sex brokers decided it was time to persuade their 'gods' to make a public appearance. At the same time, the Hernandez brothers decided to expand their scam and cash in by turning it primarily into a crooked commercial enterprise.

So off they went to Monterey in the neighbouring state of Nuevo Leon, and recruited Magdalena, the lesbian hooker with bright blonde hair, and her brother Eleazor who, like Cayetano Hernandez, was a homosexual. The homosexual brother and sister needed little persuasion to join the Hernandez brothers in their bizarre con – a con that was to turn gory and ugly.

Back in Yerba Buena, during a carefully orchestrated religious ceremony in one of the mountain caves, the Solis siblings appeared 'magically' as gods of the mountains to the naïve villagers from a cloud of smoke. No one had noticed Santos Hernandez toss a handful of flash powder on to the flames of a ceremonial brazier which stood next to the altar to the gods.

The impressionable villagers, who began attending regular ceremonies, were only too happy to provide the high priestess-goddess and her aides with their sexual favours so they could be 'purified'. The strange behaviour of her homosexual brother Eleazor was also accepted without question. After all, they were told, he was Saint Francis of Assisi.

Inevitably, the brainwashed converts were handing over their money and most precious belongings – confident that they would soon all be rich beyond their wildest dreams when the gods decided to dole out their fabulous treasures from mythical hidden caverns in the surrounding mountains.

Although the cult followers were all in it for the money, their strange cult was still strong on sex. Magdalena, the lesbian, and Santos shared the sexual favours of the young womenfolk, while Eleazor and Cayetano satisfied their homosexual lust with the able-bodied young peasant farmers. All in the name of 'purification'.

But when the promised treasures still failed to materialize, some villagers again began to get suspicious. This time, the disgruntled were promptly dubbed 'unbelievers'. Magdalena, who had won the support of the majority in her role as high priestess, fingered them as human sacrifices.

Over a six-week period, eight dissenters were beaten to death during ritual ceremonies. Incredibly, the first two 'doubting Thomases' were clubbed to death by angry neighbours fearful that unbelievers in their midst would bring the full wrath of the gods down upon their vulnerable village. To please the gods, the villagers – at the prodding of the sadistic cult leaders – drank the blood of their one-time friends and neighbours.

The six subsequent victims succumbed at more organized, sacrificial rituals, devised by the brothers Hernandez and presided over by high priestess Magdalena and her brother. The high point of the ritual was the drinking of the victim's blood which was mixed with chicken blood in ceremonial goblets.

The bizarre empire of the vampire gods began to crumble when Magdalena and Santos Hernandez became particularly besotted with a young peasant girl called Celina Salvana. Pretty young Celina had originally been Santos' steady mistress. But when the false gods came to town, Santos had generously handed Celina over to Magdalena after the prostitute-priestess cast a covetous eye over the shapely young peasant girl.

Celina went along with Magdalena's lesbian overtures at first. After all, Magdalena was supposed to be a goddess herself. But the lusty young lass soon wearied of the perverted sex and overtly expressed her preference for the masculine advances of Santos. Soon she began slipping away from the phony high priestess for romantic interludes with Santos.

Magdalena became insanely jealous. So Celina too was selected for human sacrifice. Ungallantly, Santos did not try to intercede on behalf of his fickle mistress. He did not want to take the chance of losing his exalted lifestyle.

On 28 May 1963, at a meeting of the sex cult, a terrified Celina was dragged to the ceremonial clearing by her former village friends and, at Magdalena's direction, she was bound hand and foot to a sacrificial wooden cross. Knocked unconscious by Magdalena, Celina was then beaten to death by frenzied worshippers. Brushwood was placed around the stake and Celina's body was burned, as the goddess-priestess and her cult leaders and disciples stood around chanting incoherently.

Then maddened Magdalena pointed out yet another dissenter in the assembly to her blood-thirsty followers. This time, an innocent farmer was set upon and hacked to death with machetes.

A horrified outsider – a fourteen-year-old schoolboy named Sebastian Guerrero – happened upon the sacrificial site, witnessed the madness and carnage, and ran seventeen miles to the police station in the nearest town, Villa Gran, where he hysterically reported the goings-on he had stumbled upon. Police laughed when they heard his preposterous story. But the lad, an observant and intelligent young student who hoped to be a doctor one day, was in such an emotional state that they decided to indulge him, sending a policeman, Officer Luis Martinez, with the witness to check out the story at the village.

In the patrolman's jeep, the officer and the boy headed for the mountain lair. They never returned.

Several days went by before a squad of concerned police officers and soldiers from the state capital of Ciudad Victoria were ordered to visit Yerba Buena to get to the root of the mystery. Horror-stricken, the police and soldiers on 31 May 1963, found the hacked corpses of the policeman and the boy, and grisly evidence of other killings. What was particularly shocking was that the investigating patrolman Martinez' heart had been ripped from his body.

Villagers and cult leaders scattered like the wind, most

heading for the protection of the gods in the mountains, as enraged police and *federales* raced to round up every man and woman in the village. Still convinced they had the protection of the gods, the most fanatical of the villagers holed up in several of the many caves which dotted the mountainside overlooking the village of the damned.

The brainwashed believers exchanged rifle fire with the approaching officers, wounding three policemen. But the fire power of the police and soldiers were overwhelming and the mountain cultists soon surrendered meekly.

Santos Hernandez stood his ground, but was cut down in a hail of bullets after trying to shoot it out with the police. Magdalena and her brother Eleazor were found in a house nearby, apparently totally unconcerned, both oblivious in a marijuana-induced stupor.

A head count still did not turn up Cayetano Hernandez. Police learned later that he too was dead – hacked to death by an ambitious villager called Jesus Rubio who was fed up with the homosexual cult leader's wanton ways and aimed to take over his place as one of the cult's hierarchy. Rubio, in fact, was one of the few who had cottoned on to the scam and he had killed Cayetano because he wanted a piece of the action for himself.

The Solis 'high priests' and twelve of their now sadly disillusioned followers were brought to trial on 13 June 1963. Each received prison sentences of thirty years.

JAMES P. RIVA

Man with golden bullets
drank grandma's blood

Gruesome and blood-curdling is the only way to describe the murder of seventy-four-year-old wheelchair-bound Carmen Lopez, which horrified the small town of Marshfield, Massachusetts, in April 1980. Particularly when her killer was identified as her twenty-four-year-old grandson James P. Riva II, who shot his handicapped grandmother twice as she sat in her wheelchair – using a gun loaded with golden bullets. Then, her vampire-obsessed grandson drank her blood, sucking the warm liquid through the bullet holes, before trying to cover his tracks by burning her body and her home.

The story of Jimmy Riva – an aimless drifter with relatives in both Marshfield and Jamaica Plain, Massachusetts – is truly one of the most vivid and awesome in the annals of modern-day vampires.

Jimmy was a troubled youngster who developed a blood-lust as early as his nursery school days. Later he became obsessed with the notion that his infirm grandmother

149

was a vampire predator who was robbing him of his blood as he slept. He believed that his only hope lay in shooting her – with golden bullets.

Riva's trial in October 1981, eighteen months after the horrifying slaying, and the weirdo circumstances surrounding it caused quite a stir in this normally peaceful area of New England.

Defence attorney John T. Spinale surprised no one when he announced he was seeking a verdict of not guilty for his client by reason of insanity, with a battery of psychiatrists to support this claim.

In his opening remarks, Spinale told the jury of eleven men and five women: 'During the course of the trial you will hear evidence that the defendant during his lifetime, felt he needed human and animal blood. He had a regular habit of not eating normal meals. He ate what he found in the evening, and during the evening he found animal blood.

'So the evidence you will hear goes beyond who killed Carmen Lopez. That's not the issue. The evidence is strong that Jimmy Riva killed his grandmother. But the question is: How does society handle Jimmy Riva?'

As he spoke, defender Spinale kept glancing towards the defendant's table where a gaunt-faced Riva sat, shaking silently every time his name was mentioned.

At first, assistant district attorney Henry A. Cashman – obviously aware of the pitiful and pathetic figure Spinale was painting to the jury of his client – objected to Spinale's repeated references to Riva's so-called vampire leanings.

Was it possible that Riva's obsession with vampires should not be taken into consideration as a relevant factor towards his guilt, sanity or innocence? Riva's perverse background was too relevant not to be aired openly in a court of law, decided Judge Peter F. Brady who, after a brief bench conference with the defence and prosecution attorneys, allowed Spinale to continue. The short, dark-haired defendant continued to shake visibly during his attorney's remarks.

So it emerged that the diabolical plot to slaughter his grandmother was the culmination of a whole series of bizarre incidents in the young life of Jimmy Riva.

Sadly, it was the heartbreaking task of his mother, Mrs Janet Jones – now divorced from Riva's father, the son of the victim, Carmen Lopez – to chronicle the troubled childhood of her son who claimed he feared vampires – but desperately wanted to become one.

Mrs Jones, who now lives in Middlebury, Vermont, was called as a witness for the prosecution because her son confided in her after the slaying that he was a vampire and that he killed grandmother Lopez because he needed her blood. This was at odds with another story he told investigators shortly after his arrest . . . that he shot and stabbed his grandmother because *she* was a vampire who was stealing his blood.

There was yet another motive for the barbaric killing: Riva fully believed he had become a full-blown vampire himself, and had been one for four years prior to the killing. He claimed he had kept company with other 200-year-old vampires and disembodied vampire voices were continually urging him to kill for blood. His reward for killing, according to Riva, was the prospect of eternal life. Riva honestly believed that if he killed 'everybody who was bad to him, he would come back as a handsome man and have a car and girls and his life would be fine', according to his own mother's testimony. That prospect must have been pretty tantalizing for the short, stocky, not-too-good-looking misfit with the shock of unruly dark hair and teeth stained brown from drinking the blood of cats, birds and horses.

Mrs Jones' testimony revealed how family and friends knew that everything was not all right in young Jimmy's world from the time he was in nursery school and used to shock teachers with his violent, almost surrealistic drawings. In a vivid and precocious style, the little Riva boy would spend hours with crayons carefully drawing fantasy pictures from the darker side of popular fairy tales – goblins and witches were among his favourite subjects. To this day, his mother still shudders when she recalls her little son coming home and showing off his art work for the day – 'dozens of pictures with bare bottoms with holes in them, and blood dripping on the floor, puddles of blood, and hypodermic needles'.

'We were distressed at the time,' remembers Janet Jones. 'These were scenes of violence, of guns shooting bullets, and cannons, and people dying . . .'

The child didn't just channel his latent violence into his drawings. At the age of four, he felt he had been cheated – and made a childish attempt to kill, or at the very least severely injure his father. Apparently, Jimmy's father, James Riva Sr, wanted to make change from a quarter and retrieved two dimes and a nickel from his son's piggy bank. Young Jimmy went into a rage that his father had only given him one coin, yet took three.

'We explained that they were the same amount, but he still tried to call the police. He then made a contraption with a hammer and string and suspended it over the doorway to the bedroom, so that when his father opened the door the hammer would hit him on the head,' his mother recalled.

Fortunately, the four-year-old's fiendish booby trap was discovered before anyone was injured.

And it wasn't just a phase he was going through. His out-of-this-world horror drawings continued through his lonely childhood. Then by the time he reached his teenage years, the pictures he drew took on a new, macabre sophistication. They were pictures of 'women with blonde hair with puncture wounds in their necks and blood dripping out . . . psychedelic pictures', according to his distressed mother. Tears streaming down her cheeks, a shattered Mrs Jones remembered these and other upsetting incidents from her son's childhood, as she poured out her heart to a stunned jury.

Under cross-examination by defence attorney John T. Spinale, she was unable to conceal her emotional agony as the questions got more and more painful.

Spinale: 'At that time did he begin eating strange things?'

Mrs Jones: 'He cooked up concoctions on a hot plate in his bedroom of boiled ketchup and parts of animals with oil and entrails and raw fish and birds.'

Spinale: 'Would he eat a bird whole?'

Mrs Jones: 'Yes.'

Spinale: 'Is it fair to say he constantly did this?'

Mrs Jones:'Not constantly. It was a cyclical situation.'

Spinale: 'Were there other types of behaviour?'

Mrs Jones: 'He started not sleeping at night. He'd go for days without sleeping, wandering the streets at night.'

And the entire courtroom recoiled in horror as the defendant's mother also testified that Riva, while living alone in an apartment, killed a cat and cut off its head. Then he 'dissected the brains because he said he wanted to fix his own brain'.

Spinale: 'On this occasion were there bloodstains or brown stains on his teeth?'

Mrs Jones: 'His teeth were very discoloured. They were like that for a long time.'

Spinale: 'Didn't he tell you he drank the cat's blood?'

Mrs Jones: 'Yes.'

Riva's troubled mind was whirring with esoteric fantasies. At one stage he told his parents that a spaceship had put a transmitter in his head and that the transmitter was directing his body. His distraught mother recalled how he used to wear a pyramid fashioned out of cardboard on his head because he believed 'the pyramid fixed his brains'.

Inevitably, the boy was treated at several mental institutions between 1975 and 1978. But his troubles would not go away. In fact, they became increasingly weird – so much so that his frightened relatives slept behind locked bedroom doors when he was at home. And at least one member of the family was awake at all times.

Riva was also the ultimate loner – a loner without friends, who rarely slept at night. When asked what he did with himself during these aimless years, he would answer simply that he just roamed the countryside. Like a restless vampire in search of prey?

'His behaviour became so bizarre that his family and law enforcement people were unable to determine what to do with him,' conceded his own lawyer Spinale.

It was inevitable that the young man's sick fantasies would turn to something even more horrific than the slaughter and desecration of dumb animals. The bloodlust was upon Jimmy Riva – the bloodlust of a predatory vampire.

What happened next was the subject of lengthy debate when the matter got into the hands of the courts and court-appointed psychiatrists. Did Jim Riva snap completely when he went to his grandmother's house, accosted the frail senior citizen in her wheelchair, fire two .38 calibre gold-coated slugs into her feeble body . . . then finished the job by slashing and stabbing the last breath from her body? Was it because – as he told his mother – he truly believed he was a vampire who would gain strength from supping on her blood? Or was it because – as he told a psychiatrist – he thought his grandmother was a vampire who came to sup on him as he slept? Did he think he was satisfying his masters or superiors in the netherworld of vampires by making a human kill, instead of toying around with animals? Or did he think a human sacrifice would guarantee him a life after death as a wealthy and handsome lady-killing playboy?

Only James Riva knows for sure what was going through his tortured mind as he drove up to his

grandmother's home at 19 East Street in sleepy Marshfield on that cold, rainy and blustery April day.

What is known is that he parked his car 150 feet from
his grandmother's home – all the better to gain access to
the house unseen. What is also known is that he took
time to arm himself with a knife and gun before going
calling on his grandmother – and even more time to paint
as many as nine bullets with gold paint. Then after the
vicious attack, he attempted to erase all evidence of his
crime by dousing his grandmother with petrol and setting
fire to both her and her home before cowardly and
surreptitiously fleeing the scene.

Riva's attempt to turn the homicide scene into an
accidental fire was too amateurish to fool astute police
and fire investigators who soon concluded they were
dealing with an open and shut case of murder and arson.
The bullet holes and other wounds on Mrs Lopez' badly
mutilated corpse were quickly discovered.

Detectives were intrigued by the gold-coated slugs
recovered from Mrs Lopez' body. And when firemen
discovered seven more gold-painted bullets hidden in a
metal box upstairs in the partially burned house it didn't
take long for them to put two and two together. The
discovery of matching gold bullets in the body and in the
box upstairs indicated right away it was the handiwork of
an insider, someone who knew his way around the house
intimately. And given Jimmy's track record, the bizarre
nature of the homicide led police right to his doorstep.

Despite the overwhelming circumstantial evidence,
Riva was not about to yield an immediate confession. In
fact, it took three months after the murder-arson for him

to admit orchestrating the slaying.

In spite of Riva's history of mental illness dating back to 1975 resulting in him spending time in mental institutions between 1975 and 1978, neither the police nor the jury were going to dismiss the murder of Carmen Lopez as the result of an unpremeditated act of lunacy in the light of the damning evidence of premeditation and the attempts at concealing the crime.

Nor did they believe Riva when he claimed that he fled his grandmother's home to the banks of Marshfield's North river with the intention of committing suicide – but couldn't go through with killing himself because his vampire voice advisers told him that if he did away with himself he would return from the dead as a mangled and mutilated zombie. Apparently, Jimmy the Vampire did not want to risk his undead good looks!

In the tense New England courtroom, Riva's heartbroken mother repeated the fantastic story he had told her when she visited him at Plymouth County's House of Correction two months after the murder.

Sitting forlornly behind bars, Riva had tried to excuse himself by telling his mother that he had been a practising vampire for four years and that his mystery voices had told him he had to have grandma's blood or he would die. Around the same time he had met some vampires in Florida – some of them were at least 200 years old, he said – it was they who advised him to use golden bullets to kill his grandmother – as 'they would be sure to hit the mark'.

'I thought it would take just one bullet because it was gold and would find its mark. I then tried to drink her blood because that's what the vampire told me I had to do.'

But Riva went on to reassure his mother that he couldn't drink any of his grandmother's blood because 'she was old and dried up . . . and I kept telling the voices all day I couldn't do it. Voices have told me I have to be a vampire and I have to drink blood for a long time. I've been talking with the devil for a long time. Maybe it's just in my head. I ask questions . . . and, you know, it's the devil who answers me.'

He was trembling visibly as he explained his emotions on the day of the murder: 'My brain was on fire and the voices were really bad in my head.'

After Mrs Jones' evidence about her son's dramatic jailhouse confession, assistant district attorney, Cashman rested his case without calling any psychiatric witnesses – obviously going after an uncomplicated first-degree murder conviction. Defence attorney Spinale immediately moved for a dismissal on the direct murder charge because, he said, 'The Commonwealth has failed to prove the defendant is sane.' He told Judge Peter Brady that, although the prosecution normally has a presumption of sanity, the testimony of Riva's mother clearly showed the defendant to be insane. But Judge Brady denied the defence motion.

The defence brought four psychiatrists to the witness stand during the trial, three of whom said Riva was a paranoid schizophrenic and a fourth who diagnosed him as a manic depressive with delusional mania.

The medical records over the four-year period from 1978–81 showed that Riva had had hallucinations, that he believed that most people were vampires, that he was hearing 'voices' telling him to take others' blood or he would die. All the psychiatrists confirmed that Riva told them he had killed a cat and operated on it in 1978, that he drank its blood, and that he was told to do this by a vampire.

Dr Bruce Harry of Lexington, a psychiatrist at Bridgewater State Hospital, who examined Riva on three occasions, characterized the defendant as 'a paranoid schizophrenic' who believed at the time of the murder that he had to kill his paternal grandmother because he was convinced that she, too, was a vampire, who was taking his blood while he slept at night.

Dr Harry described a schizophrenic as a person who 'hears voices giving him a running commentary of what he's doing, accusing him . . . one who finds it difficult to establish interdependent relationships . . . who believes something is wrong with his body . . . that others are trying to take something from him.' He explained that the paranoid variety of schizophrenia is 'often accompanied by the belief that there is a group of people or an organization out to get you. This is accompanied by voices. The voices will accuse you of something, verbally harass you.'

During direct questioning, Spinale asked him: 'As a result of your review of the hospital materials and your conversations and evaluation of Riva, have you formed an opinion as to his criminal responsibility?'

Dr Harry: 'Yes, sir.'

Spinale: 'Tell us what it is.'

Dr Harry: 'My opinion is that the defendant on that

day was, by virtue of mental defect, not criminally responsible for his act or able to conform his conduct to the law.'

The psychiatrist said Riva felt he had been mentally ill for some time and that there was evidence to support that he was. 'Since 1977 the defendant has heard voices telling him he should look out for other people,' Dr Harry continued. 'These are male voices. The voices are accusatory, and he believes they were persecuting him and making fun of him because he hadn't killed anyone yet. A voice told him he was a vampire and that it was necessary for him to consume blood.'

The psychiatrist confirmed that Riva had told him that on several occasions he consumed the blood of animals.

Assistant district attorney Cashman made an issue of the fact that initially Riva had pointblank denied killing his grandmother or that he was a vampire. 'Do you think it's important that the defendant parked his car 150 feet away to conceal the fact that he was in the area?'

Dr Harry: 'It may have had some relevance, but it doesn't really seem to mean anything.'

Cashman: 'The defendant indicated to you that he shot his grandmother, but Dr John Angley said in court she was shot but also stabbed. Did you believe only what the defendant told you?'

Dr Harry: 'I was concerned with the underlying motivation of concealment. He was unable to trust others.'

Cashman: 'You were relying on what he was telling you?'

Dr Harry: 'Yes.'

Cashman: 'That he's a vampire?'

Dr Harry: 'Yes.'

Cashman: 'Doesn't the burning of the body suggest to you that he was trying to conceal the murder and knew that killing his grandmother was wrong?'

Dr Harry: 'It's seductive to believe that.'

Later, Cashman asked the psychiatrist: 'You don't know whether he's fooling you when he tells you about vampires, do you?'

Dr Harry agreed he had 'no outside validation' of Riva's claims of his vampire activities, but said he believed Riva believed the tale of vampirism.

The second psychiatrist for the defence was Dr Daniel M. Weiss of Newton, who stated categorically that Riva was 'crazy'. Cross-examined by the assistant district attorney Dr Weiss said that as a result of mental disease or defect, Riva 'was unable to appreciate the criminality of his conduct or to conform his conduct to the requirements of the law.'

Cashman: 'Did the defendant tell you he wasn't a vampire at the time he killed his grandmother?'

Dr Weiss: 'He was and he wasn't. He had tasted other blood. He wasn't a real vampire. Let's say he was working on it.'

Cashman: 'Isn't it inconsistent that he feared vampires, but at the same time he wanted to be one?'

Dr Weiss: 'That's what makes him crazy.'

The third psychiatrist for the defence, Dr Mandel E. Cohen, agreed that Riva wasn't criminally responsible for his grandmother's murder, but had a different diagnosis. He said Riva was a 'manic depressive with features of delusional mania'.

'There were only two possible diagnoses: manic depressive or schizophrenic paranoid. And I favoured the first,' said Dr Cohen. 'I think he was not responsible because of that disease.' But Dr Cohen conceded it was possible for psychiatrists to argue for either diagnosis – as both showed similar symptoms.

Dr Cohen said Riva believed his grandmother was getting old and needed his blood. The doctor concluded that, in his opinion, Riva's mental state was such that he was incompetent even to stand trial.

The fourth and final psychiatrist to testify for the defence was Dr Robert F. Moore of Randolph, Mass., who told the court that Riva claimed to have first heard a 'voice' in 1977 which he believed was the voice of God. 'He was chopping down a tree in the woods with an axe and he heard a voice say to him, "Thou shalt not cut down maple trees." '

Riva had also told him that he believed all white people were vampires, 'but Negroes were not vampires, that's why they are black . . . These thoughts have stayed with him over the past four years. They come and go,' said Dr Moore.

Dr Moore's testimony differed slightly from that of the other psychiatrists in that he believed Riva was aware that killing his grandmother was wrong. But he said the defendant committed the act because he believed he would die unless he did so.

Dr Martin Kelly, a psychiatrist called by the prosecution to rebut the assertion that Riva was insane, said the self-proclaimed vampire was 'aware of wrong-doing' and 'criminally responsible' for the awful murder. Dr Kelly disagreed with the other four psychiatrists that Riva was either a paranoid schizophrenic or a manic depressive. The strongest statement Dr Kelly would make was to describe the hapless young man as having 'a borderline personality disorder'.

Judge Brady instructed the jurors that a defendant cannot be held responsible for what he has done if, because of mental illness, he lacked, first, substantial ability to appreciate the wrongfulness of his act or, second, he lacked ability to control his impulses according to the law. If that was the case, said the judge, the jurors could not find him guilty of first-degree murder, but guilty in the second degree.

After about three hours of deliberations the jury settled for the latter, finding Riva guilty of second-degree murder. He was also found guilty of arson in the burning of his grandmother's body and home, and guilty of assault and battery on a police officer when he tried to resist arrest the day after the crime was discovered.

Riva showed no emotion as the verdicts were announced.

His distraught mother, Mrs Jones, wept quietly.

Judge Brady sentenced Riva to life imprisonment in Walpole State Prison on the murder charge, and concurrently to nineteen to twenty years on the arson charge. The charge of assault and battery on the police officer was filed but not addressed by the court.

DRs TEET HÄRM and THOMAS ALLGÉN

Did vampire doctors go on a bizarre crusade to kill?

According to a sensational trial in Stockholm, diabolical doctors Teet Härm and Thomas Allgén toasted themselves in blood after murdering, then dissecting the corpse of a beautiful vice girl, as she lay on the slab of the city mortuary in Stockholm.

Incredibly, Dr Allgén's little fair-haired daughter – only two years old at the time – was present as the two evil men of medicine performed their perverted ritual which included beheading their victim with surgical power drills. Three years later the same little girl, by then a convincing five-year-old, was the witness instrumental in convicting both depraved monsters – members of a secret cult dedicated to ridding the streets of hookers.

Over a five-year period between 1982 and 1987, at least five prostitutes solicited by the prowling Dr Härm and his perverted accomplices were whisked off the streets and from seedy nightclubs in the notorious

Malmskilnadsgatan red-light district of Stockholm. Their dismembered, bloodless bodies would turn up later – carved up with surgical precision and tossed like worthless pieces of meat in fields, parks and ravines in the city suburbs.

The disappearances of several other young women – including a Japanese student, and two non-prostitutes – are also thought to be the work of the gang of vampire-like night stalkers headed by the evil Dr Härm.

From the very beginning, investigators were convinced that a maniacal medical mind was behind the senseless slaughters. They reached that conclusion because of the precise, ritualistic manner in which the bodies were carved up. The killer or killers not only had to be scalpel-trained surgeons, they had to be among the best surgeons in the land.

But Stockholm's top detectives were aghast to learn that the chief perpetrator in the murders was someone they knew very well both as a friend and valued colleague – their own senior police medical examiner, thirty-five-year-old Dr Härm, one of the world's most respected pathologists. His best friend, Thomas Allgén, a family doctor and dermatologist, was also incriminated.

It was the brutal murder of beautiful vice girl Catrine da Costa that proved the undoing of the diabolical duo. Twenty-eight-year-old da Costa suddenly went missing from the streets of Malmskilnadsgatan without leaving any trace or explanation on a warm May evening of 1983.

Sweden has a certain international notoriety as the

broad-minded world capital of free love. Nowhere is this more true than in the thriving red-light area around Malmskilnadsgatan. Catrine's fellow prostitutes noted her disappearance, but took no immediate action. Da Costa had been a hooker for ten years and her street friends assumed she could take care of herself. In any case, it was not unusual for her to take off with one of her regular clients for a few days. One fewer prostitute on the streets also meant less competition and more business for the others. That's probably the other reason why her fellow streetwalkers took their time about reporting Catrine's disappearance to the police. When they finally did, the police compiled a missing person's report, made a few cursory inquiries, then bided their time hoping Miss da Costa would reappear of her own accord.

Everyone's unspoken fears came true, however, when, almost two months after her disappearance, parts of the unfortunate Catrine's body were found dumped on the outskirts of the city. The gruesome discovery was made by a man walking his dog. He spotted a black plastic rubbish bag tossed carelessly into a clump of bushes. Investigating further, he found it contained dismembered parts of a woman's body in an advanced state of decomposition. Homicide detectives called to the scene discovered another bag in the same area, containing more body parts.

The remains were taken to the Stockholm mortuary and examined by the city's skilled medical examiner, Dr Härm. It did not take him long to re-assemble the mutilated woman – except for the head, and one breast, which remained missing.

With breezy confidence, Dr Härm was able to tell investigators that the woman had been dead for at least two months, and had probably been strangled . . . although he could not be certain of the cause of death because the head was still missing. Her fingerprints, however, had been left intact, and because Catrine de Costa was a professional streetwalker, her prints were on a police file. She was identified as the butchered, headless corpse.

Detective Inspector Olaf Hanssen, the murder expert assigned to the da Costa case, had no hesitation in declaring that Stockholm had a sexual psychopath in its midst. And his experience gave him the authority to predict that the maniac would strike again.

His grim prophecy came true a week after the da Costa discovery when another attractive lady of the night, Annika Mors, aged twenty-six, known to colleagues and clients alike as 'The Velvet Tongue', disappeared overnight.

Her remains did not take as long to turn up. Two days after her disappearance, an elderly citizen taking his constitutional morning walk in the city's Hagensten Park spotted a nude female body lying on some rocks at the foot of a small ravine. It was Annika Mors. Although she had not been dismembered like da Costa, the body was still a bloody mess. Again, the capable Dr Härm performed the police autopsy and pronounced death by strangulation.

He pointed out that the woman had been savagely tortured and mutilated before or after death. The nipples of both breasts were cut away. 'This surgery was done in a very professional manner . . . the person who did this must have medical training,' Dr

Härm coolly told Inspector Hanssen.

The doctor felt the killers of da Costa and Mors were one and the same because of the similar *modus operandi* – confirming that a sexual psychopath, a Swedish Jack the Ripper, was most definitely on the loose.

The community of hookers went into panic when a couple of weeks later, in August of that same sweltering summer, another Malmskilnadsgatan regular, twenty-seven-year-old Kristine Cravache, vanished – only to turn up a day later, naked, mutilated and strangled, under a bridge leading to the suburb of Sollentuna.

Again, Dr Härm performed the autopsy. As he was preparing his report, a delegation of terrified prostitutes converged on police headquarters demanding immediate action.

Although prostitution is not legally sanctioned in Sweden, it is tolerated much more than in other western countries. For that reason, the streetwalkers felt that the Stockholm police owed them some kind of protection.

Not only were they scared to death, their livelihood was threatened. In a matter of months prostitution had ceased to be the thriving money-making business it previously had been in the once-bustling Malmskilnadsgatan red-light area. The sex-for-sale business had dwindled to a trickle as clients stopped visiting the red-light district for fear of being interrogated by detectives investigating the murders or being targeted as murder suspects. And most of the prostitutes were turning down new clients right, left and centre. Playing safe, they were sticking to infrequent assignations with regular or known clients only.

Then, for three months Sweden's Jack the Ripper lay low. It was only the lull before the storm – events rapidly took a sensational turn.

In November, two more women, Lena Grans and Cats Falk, were reported missing. This time they weren't hookers. They were upper-class socialites – a far cry from the garishly made-up scarlet women who paraded through the Malmskilnadsgatan district in their fishnet stockings, mini skirts, spiked heels and scanty undies.

News of the two new missing women garnered more print and broadcast space and time than the disappearance of lowly streetwalkers. The stunningly beautiful Lena Grans was well-known in the capital as a party girl, a playmate and confidante of some of the country's leading industrialists and politicians. And her close friend Cats Falk made her living as a popular and attractive announcer for the state television network.

As these disappearances made newspaper headlines and were trumpeted on radio and TV news broadcasts, the Swedish Jack the Ripper investigation unit was stumped. The killer or killers covered their tracks beautifully – as if they knew every twist and turn of the murder unit's complex stake-outs and investigative techniques.

In fact, it was not until March 1985 that the bodies of Lena Grans and Cats Falk were discovered – at least their skeletons were discovered – inside Lena's car twenty feet underwater at Hamarby Dock.

Positive identification was made from the young women's jewellery and their dental work. But how they died was never fully investigated. It remains a mystery to this day and Teet Härm, who was later to be named number one suspect in their killings, is the only man alive who holds the key to that mystery. And he's not talking.

Detective Inspector Hanssen first began to suspect someone close to the police investigation was leaking privileged information when street hooker Lena Bofors came forward with an interesting theory shortly before Christmas that year. 'It's not one man,' she told Hanssen and his colleagues, convincingly. 'It's a team who have sworn to wipe us girls out one by one. I think I know who they are, and the next time they come around, I'll have names for you.'

Lena Bofors, a beautiful blonde proud of her nickname 'Big Boobs', left the police station . . . never to be seen again.

Frustrated, Hanssen and his team of detectives silently cursed themselves for not following up on Bofors' theory that there was a conspiracy-to-kill cabal stalking hookers, and for failing to keep Miss Bofors under closer surveillance. Their frustration turned to anger and anguish in January 1984 when another whore called Lota Svenson, a remarkably petite and agile twenty-year-old known as 'The Serpent', also disappeared. Like Lena Bofors, she was never seen again. Police feared the worst for both women.

Surprisingly, Inspector Hanssen got some of his best leads from his friend the medical examiner. 'It's obvious this man has a scalpel and knows how to use it,' Dr Härm told the baffled detectives. 'You don't find that kind of cutting edge on an ordinary knife,' he explained patiently. 'And he knows precisely where all the internal organs are. Which makes it easy for him to remove the heart, the liver, the kidneys or the womb.'

At last, after more than 600 prostitutes had been interviewed time and time again, police got their first promising break in the case. When their interrogations were cross-checked, the detectives found that several prostitutes had alluded to a boyish-looking, well-dressed young man who drove a white Volkswagen Rabbit. Back on the streets, they went all out to check if there was someone who could tell them more about the man in the Volkswagen Rabbit.

A timid young woman who, out of fear of what might have happened to erstwhile witness Lena Bofors, adamantly refused to give her name, told an investigator, 'Yes, I know that one. I thought he might be a photographer. He always gives you a little extra, but only after bargaining over the price. He starts out nervous. Then his personality changes completely, and he turns brutal and demanding.'

The scared young woman related how he had driven her for a sexual tryst to a quiet spot in a park near the institute for forensic medicine. He had gone berserk with her in the cramped front seat of his tiny Volkswagen after haggling over the price, and had beaten her about the face and body before having sex with her. 'I was bleeding badly, but after he had sex he just drove me home and dropped me off as if nothing had happened,' said the terrified witness.

Luckily the young hooker had not been too scared to make a careful note of her attacker's appearance, clothing . . . and, most important, the licence number of his white Volkswagen. A quick check revealed the car owner to be Dr Teet Härm.

'Our own chief medical examiner!? Impossible!' gasped an incredulous Inspector Hanssen.

Swiftly and quietly, however, Dr Härm was immediately placed under intensive police surveillance, as a background check was made on the seemingly unimpeachable city medical examiner.

A weird story that cast doubts on his character soon surfaced. A few years earlier, on 7 January 1982, Dr Härm and a young lady friend reported finding the doctor's twenty-three-year-old bride, the beautiful Anne Catherine Härm, hanging dead from the foot of her bed as they returned home.

The murder scene was a strange one – never thoroughly investigated at the time probably because of Dr Härm's impeccable reputation as one of the world's foremost pathologists. Anne Catherine's slender young body was found in a kneeling position at the foot of the bed, a dressing-gown cord tied tightly around her neck, and then tied to the foot of the iron bedstead.

The autopsy revealed death was due to strangulation due to hanging, and the death was declared a suicide. An unusual 'suicide' to say the least . . . Anne Catherine's family strongly disagreed with the conclusion, convinced all along that their beautiful young daughter was a murder victim – and that her doctor husband was the culprit.

Probing further, talking to friends and relatives of the late Mrs Härm, Inspector Hanssen and his colleagues learned that Anne Catherine was not the least suicidal prior to her premature death. There was no motive whatsoever for her taking her own life.

As far as Dr Härm was concerned, though, there appeared to be a possible double motive for Anne Catherine's death. Anne Catherine was heavily insured by a policy which also covered possible suicide. And shortly after her death, Dr Härm bought an expensive villa. She was hardly cold in her grave before widower Härm moved into the lavish new home with a new lady friend, the blonde and beautiful nineteen-year-old Christine Sorensson, who coincidentally had been his companion the night he discovered his wife Anne Catherine's body. No charges were ever brought against the doctor.

With Dr Härm's link to the Ripper murders still a closely guarded secret, detectives took to the streets again . . . this time armed with a photograph of the good doctor. Identifications were made all over the red-light district – including one particularly damning eye-witness account of how Dr Härm was seen talking to Catrine da Costa a day or so before her disappearance.

Detectives could not afford to prolong their investigation in case the dastardly doctor struck again. He was arrested in the police mortuary . . . seconds after he had completed yet another autopsy. Ranting, raving, and visibly outraged, he vehemently denied the charges.

But Inspector Hanssen was sure they had the right man. Particularly when a search of Härm's home revealed a set of bizarre photographs of his late wife Anne Catherine – one picture showed her peering anxiously through the crack of a chain-locked door, another revealed her posing nervously with a cord around her neck.

Confronted with the photographs, Härm claimed Anne Catherine had taken the photos herself, using a camera with a timer switch, a couple of weeks before her suicide. She had taken them, said Härm, to convey to him and her relatives that she was indeed planning to take her own life.

Also confiscated from Härm's home were copies of articles published by the ambitious young forensic pathologist in the world-renowned English medical journal, the *Lancet*. One article was on the subject of suicide, in particular suicide by hanging; another article was about sexual psychopaths and their perverted relationship with their victims. 'Good Lord,' exclaimed Detective Hanssen, after reading both articles. 'This man actually published studies on his crimes in a medical journal!'

Convinced though Detective Hanssen was of Härm's guilt – both of the murder of his wife and the disappearance and mutilation of goodness knows how many other women over a period of years – all the evidence against Härm was circumstantial. When the prosecutors took their flimsy evidence before an examining judge, the case against Härm was thrown out – temporarily at least. And the mad doctor was ordered released from custody on 6 December 1984.

The police, however, showed that they had no such reasonable doubts about Härm's involvement in the slayings and immediately dismissed him from his post as chief medical examiner. No official reason was given for his firing. After all, how could a man with this shadow hanging over him be allowed to continue to autopsy murder victims . . . when some of them might be his own?

Calmly but firmly protesting his innocence, Teet Härm took the dismissal in his stride. Boldly, he set himself up in private practice in Stockholm where, during 1985, he became a popular personal physician – numbering many attractive, and presumably sexually curious, young women on his list of patients.

It looked as if the Swedish Jack the Ripper case had been laid to rest when a carbon-copy Ripper mutilation-murder was reported in January 1986 in the neighbouring capital of Denmark, Copenhagen. Could Teet Härm be about to be nailed at last?

Slain and mutilated this time was a twenty-two-year-old Japanese student called Tazugu Toyonaga. Like the Swedish victims, she had been tortured and strangled before her innards were expertly removed by someone obviously skilled in surgery. It could only have been the work of one man, Dr Teet Härm, decided murder detectives in both countries. Once again Härm came under the investigative spotlight – this time by police in two countries.

But again the evidence was only circumstantial and prosecutors were not prepared to jump the gun and make a premature arrest. Once bitten, twice shy. A smug Dr Härm remained at large.

Ironically, it was not the murder of Miss Toyonaga that proved the undoing of the evil Teet Härm. It was the sad and pathetic case of a sexually molested five-year-old that gave detectives the break they had been praying for for years. The young girl in this case was little Karin Allgén, daughter of the thirty-eight-year-old dermatologist Dr Thomas Allgén, Härm's best friend and partner-in-crime.

Karin was brought to the attention of the authorities by her distraught mother, who was estranged from Allgén at the time. The psychologically disturbed little girl was believed to have been drugged and sexually molested by her incestuous father – but she had an even more horrifying tale to tell her mother and the authorities.

Her grim story came to light as she was being gently examined and interviewed by social workers at a juvenile centre which specializes in getting to the root cause of child abuse and sexual molestation. The interviewers discovered that vivid in little Karin's mind was a terrible incident that took place at the city mortuary immediately after the 1983 disappearance of prostitute Catrine da Costa.

Although she was only two at the time of the macabre murder, Karin was able haltingly to relate the horrible three-year-old murder in graphic detail – detail that could only be recounted by someone who had actually witnessed the vicious deed.

Fortunately, Karin was spared the ordeal of telling her grisly story in court during the six-week trial in the spring of 1988. Instead the little girl's evidence was played on video tape and recounted in court by her mother, social workers and police psychologists.

'They threw the head away . . . and then the lady was

177

chopped up,' the little girl's statement read.

Little Karin also described how she watched as her daddy and his friend – whom she identified as Härm – used power tools on the lady's neck until her head came off. The jury heard how the child tore the head off a plastic doll, tossed it away, then told police, 'That's what daddy did to a real lady!'

Despite strong opposition by Härm's defence counsel who questioned its credibility, the judge permitted the dramatic eye-witness testimony of young Karin Allgén to stand.

The second most damning piece of testimony against Härm came from his old pal and accomplice, the equally perverted Thomas Allgén.

For the first time, Dr Allgén revealed the true sinister motives for the red-light district murders: Dr Härm, said Allgén, had been frequenting prostitutes for years. Härm had an insatiable lust for beating up and obtaining sexual gratification from prostitutes. But he had an even more powerful and insatiable lust for blood.

Obviously, he did not feel that his bloodlust was being satisfied in his daily routine of sawing, cutting and stitching up cadavers. He wanted to be in on the kill. That's why he suddenly decided the time had come to rid the world of prostitutes, and had formed a blood-thirsty cult dedicated to exterminating ladies of the night.

Allgén claimed that he was one of Dr Härm's willing disciples in his blood brigade. And, as such, Allgén admitted his complicity with Härm in the da Costa murder. He also pleaded guilty to the incest charge

178

involving his daughter – at which the evil Härm had been present as a witness.

Allgén confirmed that the *modus operandi* of the secret sect of self-appointed vigilantes was to lure prostitutes from the streets and nightclubs to the city morgue where Härm would officiate at sacrificial ceremonies on his home ground, the mortuary slab. Their atrocities did not stop at torture and mutilation, said Dr Allgén. Blood-drinking and cannibalism were commonplace, as was necrophilia, the performance of sexual acts on a corpse. And a horrified nation heard how the brilliant Dr Härm had often been called upon to perform official autopsies on his own murder victims.

The court listened in horror as more grisly details unfolded about the evil doctor who hoarded his own private collection of human remains, including twenty human brains in a freezer, and kept three skulls – possibly souvenirs from murdered victims – on prominent display in his office.

In a glass jar Dr Härm kept the heart of his dead wife Anne Catherine whom authorities are now convinced he also murdered, faking her death to make it look like a suicide. And among his treasured possessions was a photograph of his beautiful twenty-three-year-old ex-wife, a former nurse, in her coffin.

Defence counsel attempted the *corpus delicti* defence, claiming that because Catrine da Costa's head was never found murder could not be proved beyond reasonable doubt. She could have died from other causes, argued the defence.

'If you find a young woman decapitated, you can be

sure she was murdered,' retorted prosecutor Anders Helin.

Then he further bolstered the case against Härm by producing two more incriminating witnesses. One told how he had seen toddler Karin Allgén outside the mortuary where her father worked in the company of his friend Härm. And the other witness, the owner of a camera shop, testified that Dr Allgén came into his shop to give him a film for processing. Incredibly, the film included photographs of a woman's decapitated body.

Another senior pathologist, a colleague of Härm's, said there was no doubt that Miss da Costa's decapitation was performed by someone with a skilled knowledge of pathology – a person like Teet Härm.

While Härm was only charged with the murder of Catrine da Costa, the prosecution preferring to try him on only the one case in which they felt the evidence was overwhelming, the police are convinced of his guilt in the murders of prostitutes Annika Mors, Kristine Cravache, Lena Bofors, Lota Svenson, the skeletons-in-the-car victims Lena Grans and Cats Falk, the Japanese student in Copenhagen, Tazugu Toyonaga, and his young bride Anne Catherine.

For his part, Härm professed his innocence, claiming he had been picked on by police and framed as a scapegoat so they could clear up a series of unsolved murders from their books.

In March 1988, a jury convicted Härm of the da Costa rape-murder and, with no ceremony or speechifying, he was jailed for life.

His partner-in-blood Allgén, who turned state's evidence, and was only named in the rape-murder of da Costa, and a further charge of incest with his daughter Karin, was also sent down for life.

However, that was not the end of the case. A short time after the trial, the conviction was overturned on a technicality by the Supreme Court of Stockholm. A retrial began in May 1988, and in June 1988 both defendants were found not guilty of any of the charges brought against them. Strangely enough the court, in its written sentence, found that reasonable cause existed to believe that the two doctors had indeed dismembered Catrine da Costa's body. Despite this stunning confirmation both Dr Härm and Dr Allgén were released.

ADOLFO DE JESUS CONSTANZO

Charismatic leader of bizarre drugs-and-blood sacrificial cult

A month after clean-cut American college kid Mark Kilroy was abducted by sinister thugs from the streets of a Mexican border town, his remains were found scattered around a run-down ranch on the outskirts of town.

Police on both sides of the border were horrified to discover that he had been viciously sacrificed and his body parts, blood and brains used to make mystical potions which a sadistic cult of drug smugglers believed would give them supernatural powers.

As investigators scoured the property, a run-down hell hole called the Rancho Santa Elena, near the town of Matamoros only six miles from the US border, in March 1989, they found the grisly remains of fourteen other sacrificial victims.

Heading the blood-thirsty, profiteering band of sadistic criminals was the young and handsome bisexual Adolfo de Jesus Constanzo, a Miami-born criminal and self-proclaimed psychic and cultist. As high priest of the drug-peddling blood cult, it was twenty-six-year-old Constanzo who helped select the victims for the diabolical blood rituals. Like sacrificial lambs, all the victims were sadistically slaughtered in bloody ceremonies which had their roots in Afro-Caribbean voodoo, Mexican witchcraft, and the bloodiest of Satanic rituals.

Constanzo's criminal activities and blood sacrifices stretched from Mexico City, where he lived like a king, to the impoverished areas around Matamoros, which was the jumping-off point for his large-scale drug-smuggling ring.

Constanzo's loyal and equally vicious henchmen followed his every order blindly. He even had a High Priestess – a beautiful twenty-four-year-old US physical education college student called Sara Villareal Aldrete from Brownsville, Texas – who lived a bizarre double life depending on which side of the US–Mexico border she was on.

Constanzo went under two nicknames. One was El Cubano, because of his Cuban heritage; the other was El Padrino – The Godfather. His statuesque American girlfriend Sara, as well as being his high priestess, also became The Godmother. Between them, they put the fear of death among their superstitious and less-educated underlings by claiming to possess supernatural powers and organizing frightening occult blood rituals.

Brought up against the backdrop of Santeria and Palo Mayombe, the widespread occult-based voodoo Afro-Caribbean island religions heavily into animal blood sacrifices, Constanzo was skilled in putting on believable, hair-raising occult ceremonies.

He convinced his disciple-thugs that an occult ritual known as 'escudo mágico de sangre' – the magical shield of blood – could render them invincible from threats and attacks from rival gang members, as well as making them invisible and invulnerable to arrest by police on both sides of the border during their lucrative drug-smuggling activities.

For the blood shield ritual, he gathered his followers together at their deserted-ranch headquarters. Chanting what they believed was an ancient African dialect, he blew marijuana in their faces before going on to perform blood sacrifices. To begin with, the sacrifices involved draining the blood of animals – goats, roosters, dogs, even turtles. But before long, the black magic rites required even more potent sacrifices – humans. And the Constanzo gang became a band of blood-thirsty predators.

Police believe their first human sacrifice was a twenty-five-year-old Mexican hitchhiker, whom they picked up on the road and took to the ranch, where high priest Constanzo presided over a gory, blood frenzy. He watched approvingly as his brainwashed henchmen cruelly slashed their man's throat and drained his blood into a large cauldron, the first of many such victims. How many is still a matter of speculation, although police were later to dig up the remains of at least fourteen bodies buried beneath the dusty soil in and around the notorious Rancho Santa Elena.

This vicious vampire cabal didn't come under the spotlight until the abduction of the Santa Fe student

Mark Kilroy from the streets of Matamoros, which he was visiting with fellow students for a night of fun and revelry.

The kidnapped young man was reported missing and was the subject of an intensive manhunt. He probably would have remained simply a missing person if one of Constanzo's devilish accomplices, Hernandez Garcia, hadn't been picked up by vigilant police and customs agents on another matter and, under interrogation, spilled the beans about the drug-smuggling blood cult.

Under the sweltering heat, law enforcement officers from both sides of the border accompanied a group of Constanzo's snivelling henchmen, now under arrest, to the Rancho Santa Elena where they made them dig up the remains of their victims.

It was an awful, grisly scene. Some bodies were beheaded, trussed with chicken wire. Others were totally dismembered, hearts, brains, and other vital organs wrenched from them. Others had obviously been skinned alive.

In a nearby shed other decomposed human organs were found in blood-caked vats and cauldrons. The stench around the ranch was overpowering. One of the captured smugglers, Martinez Salinas, was so overcome by the smell that he stopped digging at one point, leaned on his shovel, and begged his guard of grim-faced *federales* for a face mask. Unrelenting, they motioned with their machine guns for Salinas to continue digging, telling him: 'You did not need a mask when you buried these people.'

Mexican and American authorities were horrified as

they began piecing together the whole gory saga of 'Hell Ranch'. The story of the blood sacrifice of one kidnap victim, a fourteen-year-old boy called José Luis Garcia Luna, was particularly horrific.

A cow-herder at a neighbouring ranch, the frightened young boy was swooped on as he was innocently going about his business. A rough-textured sack was thrown over his head, and he was taken to the death ranch. Evil Constanzo gang members stood around the trembling, blindfolded youth, chanting, in candlelight. Then one of them, Elio Hernandez Rivera, the chosen executioner, stepped forward. Raising a razor-sharp machete, with one powerful blow he sliced the boy's head off.

Reaching into the head, another cult member scooped the still-warm brains from the skull and deposited them in a ceremonial cauldron. The boy's twitching body was sliced open and his lungs removed; they joined the mixture of brains and blood in the cauldron as an offering to the gods.

Mark Kilroy's sacrificial execution was just as bizarre but, hopefully, less of an ordeal. At gunpoint, blindfolded with masking tape, he was led into the sleazy shed the conspirators used as their voodoo temple.

After Constanzo, in white robes, recited appropriate, unintelligible incantations, the young American was forced to kneel. Elio the executioner stepped forward, the blade of the machete flashed, and Mark Kilroy died instantly. Some of his body organs were scooped up and mingled with blood in the ritual bowl. The cultists chanted prayers over the offering.

As Helen Kilroy, Mark's mother, was to tell a news

conference in Texas, 'I think the people who killed Mark and the others must be possessed by the devil. That's the only explanation I can think of for what they did. I pray for all of them.'

As the nationwide hunt for Constanzo and other fleeing accomplices swept Mexico, the local police were determined to erase from the map the shameful spot known as Rancho Santa Elena. And it was done in a highly unusual fashion.

After a detailed photographic record of the ranch was made for evidence, an exorcist was called to the execution site. Sprinkling salt and herbs around the property and in the foul-smelling shed, the small, brown-skinned *curandero* (Mexican mystic or medicine man) – summoned at the request of the police – said prayers and repeatedly made the sign of the cross. Then the shed of evil was doused with petrol and torched to oblivion. A wooden cross was laid on the ashes.

As the smoky cloud of supernatural evil rose near Matamoros, Constanzo and several accomplices were run to ground hiding out in an apartment in Mexico City. But they were not about to give up without a struggle. After a violent siege and shoot-out with police, Constanzo and his homosexual lover, Martin Quintana Rodriguez, were found in the apartment, their bodies riddled with bullet holes.

Five other accomplices were arrested later, including the enigmatic Sara Aldrete who vehemently protested that she knew nothing of the Matamoros ritual slayings and claimed she had been held against her will by Constanzo while he was on the run.

In the aftermath of the case, publicity about the proliferation of blood cults was rampant in both Mexico and the US. For months, it became the subject of newspaper and magazine articles, and countless television talk shows.

On one hand, indignant practitioners of voodoo and Santeria insisted that what Constanzo was up to had nothing to do with their beliefs. Their ceremonies, they claimed, involved only animal sacrifices. Constanzo had bastardized their religion into a perverted blood cult.

There are many others, however, who believe that the horror of 'Hell Ranch' stands as a warning to anybody tempted to experiment in vampire-oriented cults. 'As awful as the murders in Mexico were, maybe people here will finally open their eyes,' hoped Peggy Smith, who heads the Victims of Systems organization in Sonoma County, California. 'There's a long history of cults like this in the US – and it's time something was done about it.'

As Santeria devotees protested their religion was getting wrongly maligned, some of Constanzo's followers revealed that many of their warped rituals were based on the gory scenes from the voodoo horror film, *The Believers* – and as a result video stores along the border reported an increase in rentals of that particular film video.

Constanzo's executioner Elio, however, let the Santeros and the movie off the hook, when he confessed that the cult's practices were influenced more by the voodoo religion Palo Mayombe, described by experts as the evil flip-side of Santeria. In the loathsome African religion Palo Mayombe, torture, mutilation and the drinking of blood is commonplace, along with such unspeakable practices as necrophilia and cannibalism.

What went on at Rancho Santa Elena – and, police believe, in Mexico City as well – may well have had its roots in these Afro-Caribbean imports, but the ceremonies and rituals were undoubtedly modern-day inventions of the troubled, psycho mind of Constanzo. Incredibly, the evil legend of Adolfo de Jesus Constanzo lives on. Many of his followers today still believe their charismatic, bisexual leader was and is indestructible and that he and his lover managed to escape with their lives, leaving behind disfigured, look-alike corpses. Whatever his fate, at least one chapter in the sorry saga of the vampirish druggie cult of Matamoros has been written.

Because of complex legal manoeuvrings, High Priestess Sara and other key members of the Constanzo gang languished in a Mexico City jail for a year before coming to trial. After lengthy trials and much plea bargaining, all were convicted on charges ranging from murder, manslaughter and conspiracy to drug-dealing. All received stiff sentences – with the lightest one going to Sara Aldrete who, throughout the proceedings, maintained her claim to be a coerced victim of Constanzo, rather than a willing conspirator.

A recent incident in Ukiah, California, has reawakened the fears over such ghoulish blood cults. A group of teenagers calling themselves the Children of Death casually strolled into the county health office to ask if it was possible to get AIDS through drinking blood.

White-faced and dressed in black from head to toe, the Children of Death calmly confessed to belonging to a Satanic cult.

To compound these fears, over a two-year period in Sonoma County dozens of dead cats have been found . . . skinned and drained of blood. In the same county in 1985 two dozen decapitated goats were discovered.

JOHN CRUTCHLEY

Vampire rapist was even accused of *stealing* victim's blood

Vampire rapist John Brennan Crutchley, arrested for kidnapping a teenage girl and drinking her blood, shocked investigators when he told them he'd been drinking the blood of his wife and girlfriends for twenty years.

The case of Crutchley was unique because police actually charged the real-life Dracula with *stealing* the blood of the nineteen-year-old girl who was vacationing in Florida when she accepted Crutchley's offer of a ride – and stepped into a nightmare.

For twenty-two terrifying hours, the 5 ft. 1 in., seven and a half stone, female victim – a bookkeeper from Westminster, California – was raped and tortured in Crutchley's home in Malabar, Florida, before making a difficult escape through a bathroom window with her hands and feet manacled.

In hysterics, trembling and naked except for a large bath towel she had draped around her shoulders, she hobbled into the middle of Hall Road, a dirt road running past her evil tormentor's home. As luck would have it, an elderly neighbour happened to be driving slowly past in his old brown car. He saw the young brunette tripping over her handcuffed feet in front of him. Immediately, the passing good samaritan was out of his car and at her side. He lifted her gently in his arms and placed her carefully in the passenger seat.

That's when the young victim spoke for the first time. Trembling, she raised her bruised, handcuffed hands and pointed towards an expensive-looking red brick Colonial-style house about one hundred yards away. 'Don't forget that house,' she gasped, huddling against her elderly rescuer. 'I've been a prisoner there since yesterday morning. I've been raped. And all kinds of other terrible things have been done to me. I need to get to the police.'

Her saviour drove her to his home nearby where his wife made hot coffee and comforted the still-in-shock victim while her husband reported the kidnapping and rape to the homicide division of the Brevard County sheriff's office in Titusville.

Taken to the Regional Medical Center in the nearby town of Melbourne, the girl was treated for shock, rope burns around her neck and abrasions on her arms and legs. There were obvious signs of a recent rape.

More chilling was a doctor's diagnosis that the shocked and bewildered patient had recently undergone 'a significant blood loss' – later reported to be as much as forty-five per cent of her body's blood. She was kept in the medical centre for two days being treated for abrasions, lacerations – and severe anaemia.

Comforted by a rape victim's counsellor and Detective Robert Leatherow, the young woman haltingly but with brave confidence spilled out her story of the twenty-two hours of hell she had undergone at the hands of Crutchley.

It had all begun so innocently, she cried as she dictated a six-page affidavit about her ordeal to Agent Leatherow. It was her first-ever holiday, and she had carefully saved up for months for what she hoped would be a trip to remember.

The hitch-hiking holidaymaker said she accepted the ride in Crutchley's 1982 Datsun as she was walking through the small town of Malabar en route to visit friends in nearby Melbourne on the morning of 22 November 1985.

'I'd spent Wednesday night with a friend's mother who lives in a mobile home park in Palm Bay. When I left there yesterday morning I walked to Malabar. From there I was going to continue hitch-hiking to Melbourne where I was planning to stay over with another friend,' she stated in her affidavit. 'As I crossed the road in Malabar towards a convenience store, this guy in a Datsun pulled up alongside and asked if I wanted a ride. I had walked a good five miles from the mobile home park in Palm Bay, so I was glad to accept his offer.'

She only made her decision after eyeing Crutchley very carefully. He seemed okay to look at. She estimated he was a guy of about forty, maybe 5 ft. 10 ins. tall, with a lean build, around ten or eleven stone, clean shaven, wearing a nice-looking sports jacket – he looked every inch the respectable small town businessman and she had no qualms about accepting his offer.

It almost proved a deadly decision for her.

In the car, Crutchley seemed an easy-going, nice guy as they engaged in small talk. He told her he was an engineer in the high-tech field with a big company in Melbourne.

When the girl said she was headed for Melbourne, Crutchley volunteered to take her there. But first, he had to stop off at his home to pick up a notebook which he had forgotten to take to work with him that morning.

She agreed. Crutchley then left the main road and proceeded to drive along a series of bumpy dirt roads, past several run-down homes in seedy neighbourhoods. His companion was impressed when he drove into the driveway of his imposing home.

Parking in the car port at the side of the house, he told his passenger he would only be a few minutes, but she was welcome to come in for a drink. She refused that offer and Crutchley went indoors. When he came out, he didn't have a notebook in his hands and, for the first time, she began to worry. With good reason!

Approaching her side of the car, he said he couldn't find his notebook in the house and that it must be in the back seat of the car.

That's when he went berserk for the first time. Grabbing the passenger seat he pushed it violently forward, smashing the petite young woman against the dashboard. Half-stunned, she saw him reach into the back of the car for something. Then she felt the rough hairs of a rope noose being slipped around her slender white neck.

She made one futile attempt to fight off her attacker: 'I keep a can of mosquito spray in my purse, and I tried to get it out to use it on him. But he grabbed hold of me and told me I'd better stop resisting him or I'd get hurt. He kept pulling the noose of the rope tighter and tighter to show he meant what he said. He pulled it so tight that I passed out.'

Although she had no idea how long she remained unconscious, she knew it must have been for some time. When she came to she was in the kitchen of the house, stripped naked, spreadeagled and tied on a formica-covered counter in the middle of the room.

'I am a vampire,' the thirty-nine-year-old computer engineer coolly informed his helpless victim as he loomed over her, also naked himself, still with a firm grip on the noose around her neck. All he was wearing was a medallion on a silver chain around his neck. Choking back tears, she remembers staring at the swaying pendant, in a hypnotic, near-catatonic state of shock.

'In the background, I saw a video recorder of some kind set up on a silver tripod. I tried asking him what it was for. But every time I made a sound or motion he pulled the noose tighter,' remembered the terrified girl.

Eventually, he went to the video recorder, focused it, then raped her.

After the first brutal assault, he blindfolded his tear-stained, helpless victim. Then she felt the prick of a needle on the inside of her right arm. That was followed by the sounds of sucking. 'What are you doing?' she managed to gasp.

'I am sucking your blood. I am a vampire,' repeated the monster.

After the first blood-letting session, Crutchley untied his prisoner and allowed her to go to the bathroom. But she was so weak that she crumpled on the kitchen floor as he helped her down from the formica counter, and lapsed into unconsciousness again.

When she came to, she was trussed hand and foot again, this time with handcuffs. Crutchley told her he had to go to his office that afternoon. He locked her in the bathroom after telling her that she should not make a sound or try to escape because he had a relative with him in the house who would kill her.

She lay in the bathtub, helpless, exhausted, and totally disorientated until her evil captor returned from his place of work several hours later.

After taking off his clothes, he removed her shackles and forced her to take a shower with him. Then he raped her again – this time in his bedroom on his king-size waterbed.

While his victim was in a perpetual state of fear and shock, the demon Crutchley raped her again during the evening and night – forcing her to take a shower with him after each attack – until she eventually passed out, unable to fight off her exhaustion.

But her relentless attacker resumed his torture at around four in the morning when he awakened her with smelling salts. He raped her again. 'It was as if there was no end to it,' shuddered the tiny victim as she recounted her ordeal to the police.

After that last rape, she was lying almost lifeless when

Crutchley got the lust for blood again. He punctured her left arm with an intravenous needle which appeared to be attached to a rubber hose. She raised her head weakly and was horrified when she saw he was draining her blood through the rubber hose into a jar. When the container was half full he raised it to his lips and slurped hungrily. He quickly drained the jar.

Again, she went through the ordeal of being manacled, blindfolded with masking tape, and placed in the bathtub as Crutchley prepared to leave for his office . . . clean-cut, clean-shaven, and dressed in respectable business clothes.

Lying there alone, the girl frantically gathered her thoughts. She now doubted his story that there was a relative playing watchdog in the house. After a couple of hours, she decisively pulled the tape from her eyes, a painful and awkward process in itself.

She struggled and banged herself about as she manoeuvred her way out of the bathtub. But she didn't want to take the chance of leaving through the bathroom door, in case Crutchley hadn't really gone, or really had an accomplice in the house.

There was a small bathroom window overlooking an outside yard. This had to be her best chance. 'I figured I might just be small enough to squeeze my way through the window. I pushed the screen outward, and grabbed a bath towel from a rack,' she recalled. 'Getting out was quite a job. But I was desperate. I wriggled my body from side to side until I finally made it, falling about four feet on to the ground and freedom.'

Holding the towel around her, the unfortunate girl hobbled and crawled across the back yard, through a drainage ditch, and on to the dirt road – where she was soon to collapse into the comforting arms of her elderly rescuer.

Detective Leatherow relayed the girl's signed statement of kidnap, rape and torture to Lieutenant Thomas Fair of the homicide division. And the hunt for Crutchley was on.

That night Lieutenant Fair and a team of deputies surrounded Crutchley's home, awaiting the return of the monster. He didn't show up and the surveillance officers were beginning to think he had flown the coop until one of the deputies dived into a clump of bushes beside the house to conceal himself from the headlights of a passing truck. Incredibly, he came face to face with the fugitive – who had been hiding in the bushes himself observing the officers on their stake-out.

Crutchley at first played dumb with the officer, demanding to know why he was staking out his home. When the cautious police officer refused to tell him, Crutchley stalked indignantly into his house.

Afraid Crutchley would now try to dispose of key evidence, Lieutenant Fair went to the front door and told Crutchley he was investigating a report of a prowler in the area. Obviously nervous and suspicious, Crutchley did not invite the lieutenant into his house.

Quickly, the detectives, based on probable cause, had to get search warrants to gain access to the Crutchley home. With the help of assistant state attorney Michael Hunt, Brevard County Judge Lawrence Johnston signed the necessary papers. And at 2.37 a.m. detectives swooped on Crutchley.

Inside the house they read Crutchley his rights and told him what he was accused of. Crutchley interrupted the officers and retorted, 'I know why you guys are here. You don't have to read me all that stuff. I screwed up. I messed up. But I want to tell my side of the story.'

At police headquarters, Crutchley was given the services of attorney Rick Singer, the public defender on duty, whose initial advice to the accused was to keep his mouth shut until the full facts of the girl's allegations had been investigated.

Crutchley neglected to take his lawyer's advice. And the weird story he told was totally at odds with the girl's account – and nearly as bizarre.

After he picked up the hitchhiker, said Crutchley, she asked him if he had any drugs. That's when he noticed the initials 'C.M.' tattooed on her neck. 'I assumed then that she was one of Charlie's girls,' Crutchley told the police.

Asked who he meant by Charlie, Crutchley said he was referring to Charles Manson, the notorious convicted killer and cult leader.

His sexual relations with the girl began after she told him that she had kinky fantasies about being strangled. 'She was sitting in the car begging . . . she wanted it to be rough,' alleged Crutchley.

That's when he got carried away and began choking her before dragging her into the kitchen where they had sex after he tied her to the kitchen counter. Crutchley kept on insisting to the disbelieving interrogators that the girl was a willing participant to the bondage and the sex.

'When it was over she asked me about other sado-masochistic practices, including the use of handcuffs. I realized I had got myself into a hell of a mess. I decided to take blood from the woman. I'd been introduced to that practice a few years ago by a nurse in Washington, D.C.,' continued Crutchley in his statement to the police.

As he gave his warped version of the sordid events, including details of his other kinky sex acts, he fidgeted constantly in his seat. Detectives observed that his mood swung between sad and happy, sometimes crying as if racked by guilt, sometimes laughing as if he enjoyed the retelling of his story.

Asked what he had done when he found the girl had escaped, Crutchley told Lieutenant Fair, 'I freaked out. I'd gone home for lunch, and when I saw she wasn't there I got frantic. I gathered up her clothes, some IV needles, and the bloodstained jar. I erased the videotape of the sexual encounter in the kitchen. I stuffed everything into the oversized purse she had been carrying. I had to go back to work. I drove north to Melbourne . . . and threw the articles on the roadside for a stranger to pick up. I can show you where I threw them.'

Detectives raced to the scene, but could find no trace of the victim's purse or the other articles. They were, in fact, never found.

As the strange, spine-chilling story of Malabar's own Count Dracula hit the headlines in Florida in November and December 1985, psychologists and investigators probing the background of John Brennan Crutchley – who had managed to get himself freed on $50,000 bail – found they were dealing with a truly enigmatic character.

Born in Pittsburgh to a well-to-do family, John Crutchley graduated from high school in Pennsylvania. He later earned a bachelor's degree in physics at Defiance College, Ohio, going on to gain a master's degree in engineering administration at George Washington University in Washington, D.C.

Everyone thought of him as a loner-genius. As a kid he seldom played with others, preferring to spend most of his childhood years tinkering with electronic gadgets in the basement of the family home.

Like a lot of kids he did a paper round, but in his teenage years he earned considerably more extra money by repairing and rebuilding complex radio and stereo systems. Schoolmates, teachers and early employers can only remember him as 'young John, the computer whizz-kid'.

After he graduated from college in 1970, his year-old marriage began falling apart. It collapsed completely when he went to Indiana to start his first job. He moved to Fairfax, Virginia, in the 1970s, remarried, but that union, too, soon fell apart. He married a third time in 1980, had a son, but uprooted to move to Malabar in 1983.

His third wife, Karen, and son were out of state visiting relatives at the time of his arrest. He was, however, still working at his key $50,000 a year job – designing hush-hush programs – with the prestigious Harris computer and electronics company in Melbourne.

The first clue to the dark side of the three-times-married, twice-divorced loner-genius with the warped personality came when police did a thorough search of his Malabar home. There they discovered a collection of leather dog-type collars, chains, needles, rubber hoses, a video recorder and a number of video tapes. Also in the house were identification cards in different names, twenty grammes of marijuana, and the strangest find – bags of brown and blonde hair clippings.

The identification cards were in women's names. Two of them were traced to Crutchley's first wife to whom he was married between 1969 and 1973, and the third was traced to his second wife with whom he had lived in Indiana and Virginia in the 1970s.

When contacted, one of the ex-wives told the detective: 'John had a violent temper and scared me a lot. But he never did anything this kooky. He must have really flipped!'

Then police began getting information about Crutchley from other law enforcement agencies which raised their hackles.

Shortly before Christmas 1985, Lieutenant Fair got word from Fairfax, Virginia, police that Crutchley was well-known to them. In fact he had been under close scrutiny by them after the disappearance of a twenty-five-year-old woman named Deborah Fitzjohn in their area in 1977. Her bones were eventually discovered by a hunter in 1978 nine months after her disappearance – and Crutchley was questioned several times about his possible involvement in her disappearance and murder because he was known to be Miss Fitzjohn's boyfriend and she was last seen alive at the trailer park where Crutchley lived.

The police began to worry – did they have a sick serial killer on their hands, instead of a sick, kinky computer buff?

After studying the Fairfax evidence, Brevard County state attorney Norm Wolfinger ordered a report on all missing women in his county since Crutchley's arrival in the area in 1983.

That probe produced a dossier on six missing women, of which the skeletons of five had been discovered in deserted areas in southern Brevard County. Two of the skeletons had been identified – those of Kimberly Walker, aged twenty-one, of Vero Beach, and forty-year-old Lynn Kay Desantis of Melbourne. But three others – found in the Malabar–Palm Bay area – had not.

The sixth, still-missing woman is Patti Volanski of Scottsmoor, Florida, whom Crutchley admitted picking up in his car in March 1985. Her wallet was found in his car, but Crutchley claimed Volanski was alive and well after he dropped her off.

One of the few slender clues in the Florida disappearances was that another one of the missing women was last seen getting into a small, light-coloured car. At that time, Crutchley was the owner of a compact, beige Nissan Stanza.

Taking all things into consideration, state attorney Wolfinger filed a motion in the courts to have Crutchley's bail bumped up from $50,000 to $500,000. The court agreed, and the high bond was effective in getting Crutchley off the streets and behind bars by early

January 1986, to await his April trial.

At that time, a very subdued Crutchley made a brief appearance before Judge John Antoon in Titusville, Bible in hand, claiming that he had a spiritual experience in his jail cell. 'I was at the bottom of an emotional pit . . . I had no meaning in life,' he explained, announcing his religious conversion to the court.

By then rumours about the existence of a Count Dracula in Malabar and all kinds of speculation about his nocturnal activities were rampant in Brevard County. Fearing that his chances of getting a fair trial were being torpedoed by hearsay and innuendo, Circuit Court Judge John Antoon imposed a gag order prohibiting police and lawyers from talking or releasing information about the case. But he refused a request by Crutchley's defence council, Joe Mitchell, to change the venue of the upcoming trial because of the widespread, pre-trial publicity.

There was, however, an upsurge in the furore surrounding the case when, a couple of weeks before the trial date, state attorneys slapped Crutchley with two additional charges – one of *stealing* his victim's blood, and another of more serious sexual battery because of the violence he had shown to his victim.

Crutchley was to face a judge and jury on no fewer than twelve charges including kidnapping, several counts of sexual battery, theft of blood and possession of marijuana.

'This is just too bizarre,' protested Crutchley's lawyer Joe Mitchell when he heard about the blood theft charge. 'I'm sure there's never been a case before in

Florida, or the whole country for that matter, where if you take someone's blood, it's robbery!'

State attorney Wolfinger was inclined to agree: 'I've never prosecuted anyone for stealing someone's blood before.' But he added: 'The victim claims Crutchley literally stole her blood against her will, and blood has value – so that's serious robbery.'

After this new wave of sensational revelations, Judge Antoon had little choice but to agree to a change of venue, from Titusville to Gainesville.

These desperate efforts by the defence did not stop the mounting wave of evidence against Crutchley, though.

Two Brevard County jail cell-mates, Patrick Dontell and Gregory Raub, came forward to say that Crutchley had confided to them on separate occasions that his kidnap victim was lucky to be alive . . . that he had intended to kill her had she not escaped. Police also had evidence that Crutchley had admitted that the prisoner Dontell and himself were like brothers and that he had told him 'everything'.

State attorney Wolfinger claimed that Crutchley's bizarre appetite had earned him unwanted notoriety while he sat in jail awaiting trial. 'Instead of Count Dracula, the other prisoners have named him Count Malabar,' said Wolfinger. And he added that, regardless of any jail time on the kidnap-rape, investigators would not rest until they compiled enough evidence to charge Crutchley with at least six other murders, in which he remains the principal suspect.

By now, Crutchley's lawyers were in the market for

plea bargaining – although Crutchley himself said he wanted to plead guilty to 'spare that frightened little girl out there' the further ordeal of getting into the witness box and publicly testifying against him. The prosecution agreed to drop eight other charges – including that of theft of blood – if he would plead guilty to kidnapping and three charges of sexual battery. The offer was accepted.

In court, psychiatrist Dr Ralph Greenblum presented a psychiatric report on Crutchley which read in part: 'Sexual sadism is a primary diagnosis . . . sadistic fantasies are quite common in these individuals and certainly Mr Crutchley has a long history of these fantasies.' Dr Greenblum said that Crutchley's wife Karen even described him as having always been 'a little weird'. She felt that he was heading for some kind of breakdown.

These thoughts were echoed by his mother Mildred who said after the guilty plea, 'Something snapped. It just had to. I just can't believe it of John. The only problems we ever had with him was getting him to eat when he was a baby, and getting him to study when he was at school.'

On 23 June 1986, in Titusville, Crutchley's guilty plea was accepted and he was jailed for twenty-five years on one count of sexual battery, followed by fifty years' probation.

Although Crutchley's defence blamed the accused's preoccupation with pornography for his obsession with weird sexual rituals, Judge Antoon told Crutchley as he handed down the stiff sentence: 'The nature of the crime was a grotesque demonstration of utter disregard for human life.'

Crutchley appeared unusually unruffled and composed as the judge passed sentence, but it was a different story when he was returned to his jail cell.

'I guess he was surprised at his sentence,' Sergeant Elizabeth Canada, the county jail supervisor, observed later. 'We had to restrain him physically to keep him from beating his head against the bars of his cell. He was very upset and temporarily lost control of himself.'

As a result, Crutchley was placed on suicide watch in an observation cell where he could be checked on every five minutes.

Dogged prosecutors and police investigators have not closed their books on the diabolical Crutchley although under current guidelines, the vampire rapist could be due for release as early as 1993.

At the time of writing, police and prosecutors in Brevard County are still keeping open the unsolved murders of young women in Florida and Virginia. Crutchley, concedes his former lawyer Mitchell, is still the prime suspect in these killings and was at one time ready to make plea bargains on as many as six unsolved murders – but the deal with the state prosecutor fell through.

Recently, state attorney Wolfinger revealed that the prosecution's strategy all along was primarily to get Crutchley off the streets and into prison so they could continue building up iron-clad cases against him for the unsolved homicides without relying on plea bargains. 'There comes a point when the state has to show something. And if we had anything to tie a charge to, we would have done it. But we had nothing. But we will continue to work on these cases as hard as we can,' said the prosecutor.

INDEX